HOLLYWOOD
AT
SUNSET

Books on Film

Hollywood in the Forties (with Joel Greenberg)
The Celluloid Muse (with Joel Greenberg)
Hollywood Cameramen: Sources of Light
The Films of Orson Welles

Poetry

A Distant Star
Spring and Death
The Earthbound
Noonday Country
The Voyage to Brindisi

Anthologies

They Came to Australia
Australians Abroad
Penguin New Writing in Australia

Charles Higham

HOLLYWOOD
AT
SUNSET

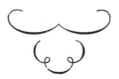

Saturday Review Press
New York

Published simultaneously in Canada by
Doubleday Canada Ltd., Toronto

Library of Congress Catalog Card Number: 78–182474
ISBN 0–8415–0152–1

Saturday Review Press
230 Park Avenue
New York, New York 10017

PRINTED IN THE UNITED STATES OF AMERICA

Design by Margaret F. Plympton

Acknowledgments

Over the years the following people have been immensely helpful in supplying material that has formed part of the substance of this book:

Leopold Friedman, Sy Seadler, Bette Davis, Irving Rapper, Spyros Skouras, Francis Ross of the Chase Manhattan Bank, former Attorney-General Tom Clark, Herbert Biberman, Hedda Hopper, Walt Disney, Dalton Trumbo, Albert Maltz, Ring Lardner, Jr., John Howard Lawson, Adrian Scott, Seymour Peck, Milton Gunzburg, Julian Gunzburg, J. Peverell Marley, Earl Sponable, Sol Halprin, Jean Negulesco, Joseph Vogel, Stanley Scheuer, Leon Shamroy, Rouben Mamoulian, Ranald MacDougall, Benjamin Thau, Stephen Boyd, Robert Surtees, Charlton Heston, Joe Canutt, William Wyler, Sol C. Siegel, Lewis Milestone, Arthur Knight, Marlon Brando, Jerry Lewis, Hal B. Wallis, Taft Schreiber, Ross Hunter, Paul Kohner, Robert H. O'Brien, Ted Flicker, Arthur Miller, Curtis Harrington, and officials of MCA/Universal and the William Morris Agency who have preferred to be nameless.

I am also most deeply grateful to the staff of the Academy

of Motion Picture Arts and Sciences Library, to DeWitt Bo-
deen, Art Murphy, Ann Bloch, Joel Greenberg, and to my
editor, Steven Frimmer, for valuable help.

Factual material has been drawn from contemporary newspapers and magazines including *The New York Times, Time,
Newsweek, Life, Fortune, The Hollywood Reporter, Variety,*
and *Films in Review,* which was particularly helpful on the
history of 3-D films.

HOLLYWOOD
AT
SUNSET

1

Nineteen forty-six was the biggest year in Hollywood's history. The gross box office receipts in that extraordinary twelve-month period were $1750 million. During the three and a half years that America had been involved in World War II, audiences had flocked to the movies. It was not just a habit, it was a compulsion. Women on the home front, dogged by the strain of worrying about their husbands or sons, had developed movie-going to an extent unprecedented since the birth of talkies. Men at war, with jungle, desert, or shipboard showings virtually their only diversions, had created a new generation of pinup girls, led by such figures as Betty Grable (the top box office star in 1943) and Rita Hayworth.

Those were the uncool days when the star system was at its Technicolor zenith, when millions identified with or worshiped the glamorous figures of the screen. In 1945, Bing

Crosby, currently typecast as priests, was the first male favorite; Greer Garson, genteel, ladylike, was the most widely admired female star. Thousands of fan letters a month poured into the letter boxes of popular figures like the tiny, ineffably cute Margaret O'Brien, the perennially suffering Joan Crawford, the spunky Bette Davis, and even such now forgotten figures as John Lund, Arturo de Cordova, and Sonny Tufts. Many stars engaged secretaries to answer the flood of correspondence and provide facsimiles of their signatures, while the secretaries of those who were slipping provided some of the letters as well.

Nineteen forty-six was an innocent year, in terms of popular taste—though the makers of the gilded pap that passed for entertainment could scarcely have been called innocent. They had retained the native cunning which they had brought into the film industry back in the teens of the century when they had come out of Russia or Poland via the garment jungle into the theater business to control motion pictures, to sell unknown shopgirls and soda jerks as stars who invaded the world's dreams. Seemingly the entire female population followed Hollywood's lead when Veronica Lake let her hair fall in a peekaboo style, creating factory problems when long hair caught in machinery. Girls piled their hair high when Betty Grable piled hers, let their skirts fall low when Maureen O'Hara sported low-cut skirts in *Do You Love Me?*, painted their mouths in wide gashes and sported wide, padded shoulders when Joan Crawford appeared in *Mildred Pierce*.

Women's fashions of 1946 still spell nostalgia: pocketed skirts and ribboned hair, anklestraps, platform-soled shoes, hats like mushrooms or pill boxes. The music popular then was apt to be loud, harsh versions of boogie-woogie or bebop, and not even the most elevated stars dared ignore it: a jitterbugging GI had thrown Bette Davis around his head in *Hollywood Canteen* and she even sang a song that went:

"I'll never never failya/ When you are in Australia/ Or out among the Russians/ Or off in the Aleutians."

When stars went to premieres they were liable to be stripped, have their hair pulled or their arms bitten. When Barbara Stanwyck traveled to London for the opening of her film *The Other Love,* a woman sank her teeth in her ankle and would not let go until pried loose by police. When Van Johnson went to a store to sign photographs in 1946, he was thrown to the floor and almost trampled to death. When *Northwest Mounted Police* was shown earlier in the forties, 12,000 women entered a world competition, the prize for the winner being the opportunity of sitting next to Gary Cooper at the Chicago opening. The gossip columnists, led by Hedda Hopper and Louella Parsons, were syndicated in hundreds of domestic newspapers, imparting such crucial information as that Tyrone Power had almost been in a wreck on a South American cruise, Gene Tierney was having marital problems with dress designer Oleg Cassini, and Myrna Loy protected her peach tree from unseasonable frost by swathing the trunk in her mink. The Hollywood historian Leo Rosten wrote: "One dare not speculate on the avidity with which readers devour such news items as Norma Shearer's alleged purchase of $1,000 worth of handkerchiefs for Christmas presents, the gesture of George Raft in ordering 21 champagne cocktails for the barbers and beauty operators while he had his hair cut. . . . [The] idols of the screen are an international royalty whose dress and diet and diversions are known to hundreds of millions of subjects."

Photoplay and the other mass circulation fan magazines carefully sustained the public illusion of Hollywood, since the hard-drinking, whoring reality would scarcely have interested a naïve mass audience. Although Dorothy Parker's description of Hollywood as a woman with a white suede glove holding a bagel with a bite out of it still made sense, the public wanted to imagine nothing but the stars splashing happily up and down in their pools or stretching their golden limbs as they awaited the arrival of a chocolate milkshake. To the rest of the Western world, Hollywood was Paradise, something to think about as you stood in line for rations in the rain.

When the war ended, and the stars were demobilized, war stories became rapidly taboo. A few films—most notably William Wyler's enormously successful *The Best Years of Our Lives*—showed the adjustment of soldiers to peacetime life, but this was rare. In the Atomic Age, audiences wanted even more escapism than they had demanded during the war: among the great successes of that period were *Margie,* a story about college life in the 1920s, *Blue Skies,* a musical with Fred Astaire and Bing Crosby, and *Deception,* in which the most serious question was whether Paul Henreid would complete a performance of a cello concerto before its composer–conductor Claude Rains was shot dead by Bette Davis. In those days the most eagerly required sight was of the kind *Life* magazine commented on: "Greer Garson, scrambling eggs in an anteroom of the Taj Mahal."

The star system, established from the outset of the cinema, was based on contractual employment of figures which gave a studio the image it wanted. Paramount wanted lightheartedness, MGM sentimental saintliness, Warners toughness, 20th Century-Fox a sophisticated gloss, Universal a pioneer briskness, Columbia ritziness; and Garson, Bogart, and Bacall, Gene Tierney, Yvonne DeCarlo, Rita Hayworth, and the other stars provided embodiments of these images.

Stars themselves, along with their wealth, their opulent homes and their huge cars, lived strenuous lives. Up at 5 A.M., they would drive long distances to the studios where makeup men would labor to expunge every wrinkle and line, and make sure that their lips and eyes exactly conformed to the public's requirements.

At seven or eight they would be on the sound stage steeling

themselves for sixteen or more takes of a kissing or shooting scene. Late at night, exhausted and depressed, they would go home, soak in a hot tub, and go to bed. They were geared utterly to this gruelling existence: if they were dropped by a studio, life seemed empty and meaningless and they took to drink, gambled, lost their money, or left Hollywood altogether, as dead professionally as yesterday's fashions, condemned finally to become objects of camp cults.

That was a cheerfully extravagant period. A director like William Wyler could still consume all the time he liked over a picture and shoot dozens of takes to ensure a perfect result. The late Sam Wood shot 600,000 feet of film to make a 15,000-foot feature, *Saratoga Trunk,* and even then it was overlong and dull. Wastage was severe, but the pictures often looked rich and splendid as a result. Arthur Miller, Academy Award-winning cameraman, spent $20,000 of the studio's money on buying new lenses and spraying the furniture with oil to ensure a glistening look for *The Razor's Edge* and *Anna and the King of Siam,* while Leon Shamroy spent virtually the same amount to ensure glamor for a life of Wilson. In one scene—the Baltimore Democratic Convention of 1912 shot in the Los Angeles Shrine Auditorium—he filled the building with four hundred arc lights to show five thousand people with equal clarity in perspective.

Extravagance extended to the lives of the tycoons who condoned it. The studio heads lived like Renaissance princes with homes in Europe and in Beverly Hills, servants, limitless access to beautiful women, large cars, and mountains of shares and bonds. The most powerful figure in Hollywood was Louis B. Mayer, spectacular head of the greatest studio —MGM. Mayer's studio was the finest, boasting—to quote a celebrated publicity line—"more stars than there are in heaven" and, as the chief selling point of its postwar demobilization picture *Adventure,* "Gable's back and Garson's got him." A driveway such as might have rolled up to Tara or Twelve Oaks in *Gone With the Wind* rolled up to the classic white façade of the Irving Thalberg building, the pretty secretaries, well-tailored executives, and handsomely appointed offices providing perfect fronts to impress the visiting journalist. The commissary was crowded with famous names at lunchtime, and eating Louis B. Mayer Chicken Soup (a favorite of his mother's) was virtually obligatory.

In 1946, with salaries still curtailed by a wartime wage-freeze, Mayer was one of the highest paid men in the country, earning $249,048 a year. *Fortune* called him "perhaps the most feared man in Hollywood" and *Current Biography* said of him: "If George Bernard Shaw or Albert Einstein visits Hollywood it is Mayer who will entertain him, engage him in intellectual discussion, and introduce him to Mae West." To the world of intelligent people who knew little about the making of films, Mayer *was* Hollywood.

He was a short, broad man, smiling frequently but capable of powerful outbursts of rage. His size was a worry to him; when a well-known star walked into his office for the first time, saw him behind his huge desk, and said, "Don't you normally stand when a lady enters the room?" he snapped back, "Madam, I *am* standing." He had an unequalled instinct for selecting stars. While touring Europe he saw photographs of Garbo and signed her up at once without even meeting her, and he signed Judy Garland to a contract without even subjecting her to a screen test. He followed his instinct to the end, supplying the public with grandiose, lavish escapist entertainment laden with *schmältz*.

Born in 1885, Mayer was a Russian Jew (when a star is said to have complained about the number of Jews running around the studio his reply was, "Madam, what do you think I am, a Hibernian?"). He came to America as a child via Canada. One of his first jobs was salvaging iron from sunken ships; he sold the scrap iron at a profit, and while on a trip to Boston saw possibilities in newfangled movie shows. In

1907 he bought a former burlesque theater in Haverhill, Massachusetts, and set the tone of his career by opening it with *From The Manger to The Cross*, a primitive Bible-in-Pictures religious film. Learning about *The Birth of a Nation*, Griffith's recently produced epic in 1915, he obtained the exclusive rights to show it in New England. In 1924, after merging his own company with Nicholas Schenck's outfit, he became vice-president in charge of production, a position he retained thereafter.

He usually rose at seven o'clock and at 8 A.M. began his calls from home to the New York office, reporting on the previous day's activities. After an hour of golf he drove to work at about 11:30 A.M., weaving his way recklessly through traffic from his home in Santa Monica to the studio in Culver City. At his office, a resplendent room designed by the art director Cedric Gibbons, he worked almost without interruption until 9 P.M., refusing to permit his secretary to open any mail, dealing personally with stars. He was capable of singing to a Judy Garland or a Jeanette MacDonald to show them what they should do with their voices, and once gave Mickey Rooney a lesson in how to cry.

Mayer had a happy home life with his wife and daughters, and later when the two girls married into the industry—Irene to David O. Selznick and Edith to William Goetz—he was very proud. He owned racing stables, loved to rhumba when the craze was on, and was obsessed with pinochle. He was seldom known to read a book—unless the author was on his way to Hollywood as a V.I.P. He detested "intellect" on a higher level than James Hilton.

On the surface, Louis B. Mayer was a happy man in 1946, limitlessly wealthy, powerful, world-famous. Yet he had an agonizing worry about which few outside of the industry had so much as an inkling. He knew that his power could be snatched away from him at a moment's notice, that all his vast influence was largely an illusion. For he wasn't, as the

(9)

world thought, an autonomous giant; he was an employee as dismissable as the humblest janitor. He was under the thumb of a man who in truth was his superior, his ruler. That man was Nicholas Schenck.

2

While Louis B. Mayer was the world-famous figure, the star-maker and movie tycoon *par excellence,* Schenck was the obscure, quiet manipulator of the strings that made Mayer work. Nobody knew this fact outside of the industry (few were even aware of Schenck's existence), and Schenck enjoyed preserving his absolute privacy. As president of Loew's Incorporated, the parent theater company which controlled MGM from New York, he was perfectly happy to see Mayer bask in the spotlight. But if Mayer elected to create a project without consulting Schenck first, or should he fail at the box office with any given film, Schenck would haul him over the coals as brutally as any messenger boy.

Schenck was born in 1882, which made him three years older than Mayer. He had a similar background: his parents were poverty-stricken immigrants who had fled Russia after a pogrom when Schenck was about seventeen years old. With his brother Joe he went into the pharmacy business in New York, finally owning their own shop, and peddling illegal drugs on the side. They plunged their early savings into an investment in an amusement park at Fort George, a short trolley ride from New York, where Schenck married a buxom cashier, a woman whose name was never made public. Later, when she became an embarrassment to his career, he shed her at a reputed cost of a million dollars.

The Schenck brothers moved in and set up the Palisades Amusement Park. Later, Schenck went into the theater business, along with Marcus Loew, and together they established a chain, Loew's, Inc., which merged with the Samuel Goldwyn and Louis B. Mayer companies in the early 1920s, giving Schenck absolute power following Marcus Loew's death in 1926.

Schenck was an iron-carapaced puritan who shared Mayer's sentimentality, his shrewd assessment of the public's needs, and his showman's flair. Oddly enough, both men were almost exactly the same height, about five six and a half in their stocking feet, and both had owlish, pink, Russian faces with eyes that crinkled when they laughed. Schenck's shoulders were like Mayer's—thick and broad—and he had the kind of massive limbs and trunk needed to carry the burdens of executive office. He could look charming, his quizzical brown eyes peering through professional horn-rims, his fresh complexion glowing after a visit to the race track. Like Mayer, and like many immigrant Slavs of his class, he feared and mistrusted intellectuals and sophisticates, and he had an atrocious temper when crossed by one of that breed. He had a grudging respect for Irving Thalberg but never really liked him; to Schenck, Thalberg's middlebrow "intellectualism" seemed loftier than a Bertrand Russell's. Later, he had an uneasy relationship with Dore Schary, the playwright and "liberal" middlebrow brought in to Metro-Goldwyn-Mayer in the late 1940s to be head of production.

Schenck was fanatically shy, secretive, and removed, chiefly because he hated to show his lack of any formal education to people he thought might be more intelligent or informed than he. His Russian accent, never shed, infuriated him; he was annoyed, too, that voice coaches had carefully eliminated Mayer's. He hated and feared reporters and never gave an interview in case something he said might appear stupid or illiterate in print. In common with Mayer, who heartily disliked him, he was a hypochondriac, guarding himself against illness by constant visits to physicians, sending aid to an unwell staff member in the form of various nostrums, but, if the disease might be catching, failing to visit the patient himself. When Mayer fell sick with leukemia in the 1950s, Schenck was beside himself in case the same fate should befall him. Yet until his final decline—he became increasingly senile, talking in a thin, piping voice at public gatherings—he never had a sick day in his life.

Schenck's only two concerns outside of his consuming passion for the company were his second wife, Pansy, a former Southern belle, whom he adored, and horses. Unlike Mayer, he did not buy horses, but he loved them and betted on them obsessively, often traveling to the Miami racetrack to follow a particular hunch.

His wealth was immense and scrupulously invested, both in and out of the company. His income was about $650,000 per annum during his last years of office, and what little he reserved for his personal use was spent on maintaining his comfortable home at Port Washington, Long Island. His needs were simple and his wardrobe of gray suitings not large. He maintained the frugal uncomplicated life of a humble Russian *petit bourgeois,* and he was extremely puritanical. He was never known to make a pass at a secretary or speak in the foul language of his counterparts on both coasts, and he detested anything even faintly immoral in his company's films. In 1946, his board of directors was extremely conservative, chosen from personal friends. He demanded absolute uniformity of purpose, unswerving loyalty and yea-saying among both his directors and every one of his employees. Arguments or even discussions of policy did not interest him in the slightest: his word was law. If crossed even in the most trivial matter he would fly into an hysterical rage. The instant his subordinate was cowed into agreeing with him, he would become calm again. It was not that he was without charm or kindness, it simply never occurred to him that he could ever be wrong, and he would hound a dissenter pitilessly.

In New York, his executives were never permitted the luxury of putting pressure on him for changes. His vice-president and office treasurer, Charles Moskowitz, was like a shadow of Schenck himself, obeyed by everyone. Arthur Loew, the son of Marcus, as quiet and subdued as Schenck himself, was next in the hierarchy. Other vice-presidents included J. Robert Rubin, who had been Schenck's favorite since the thirties and was used to discipline Mayer, Alexander Lichtman, Samuel Katz, the polished lawyer Leopold ("Lep") Friedman, the publicity chief Howard Dietz, the cold-hearted theater treasurer Joseph R. Vogel, and Schenck's nephew, Marvin. The board of directors included these names and several others respected in the business world—Henry Rogers Winthrop, William A. Parker, and Eugene W. Leake. There were thirty-five department heads and a staff of hundreds in New York as well as the massive ramifications of the Loew's International Organization.

Schenck's attitude to film-making handed down to his employees was unswerving. He believed that the American public, weighed down with the problems of life in a complex urbanized society, saddled with bills, debts, and all the other agonies of daily existence, wanted escape pure and simple when they went to the movies. He saw to it that MGM surpassed all other studios in the glamor of its stars, in the escapist romanticism of its stories, in the luxury of its clothes and settings, and in the vividness of its false portrayal of history. For years, all the other studios followed suit.

Until the late 1940s, Schenck's policy executed so efficiently by Mayer was extremely fruitful. But he failed to see that the days of "his" kind of picture were numbered, and that television was just over the horizon. His tragic mistake—and his shortsighted action later in instituting on behalf of the banks the Hollywood blacklist, which stripped Hollywood of its Left Wing intellectuals for more than a decade—finally brought about the downfall of the very empire he had so patiently and relentlessly built up over more than a quarter of a century.

No other studio heads had the immense and irresistible influence of Schenck and Mayer, and most were content to follow their general production policies. Barney Balaban was head of Paramount. Adolph Zukor, who had founded the Famous Players Company which gave Paramount birth in 1912, was now in his seventies, acting chiefly in an advisory capacity while Balaban handed down the decisions in New York. Balaban, a conservative, dry man, was an expert in money matters and had made his name with the famous Balaban and Katz theater chain which he helped to found. Everyone wanted to work for Paramount, because it was devoid of the severe tensions of the other studios. It was run by an enlightened if rough and money-minded production chief, Y. Frank Freeman. Paramount films, made in the tradition laid down by Ernst Lubitsch, were light, polished, of a glossy MGM glow; but occasionally Balaban and Freeman, unlike Schenck and Mayer, would permit a change of pace: a *Lost Weekend,* or later on, a *Sunset Boulevard.*

Warners was a very different studio from Paramount. Jack Warner, who ran the production end in Hollywood, was, unlike Freeman and Mayer, answerable to no one when it came to making production decisions, his brothers Harry and Albert concurring with him in almost every move he made. Brashly humorous, skilled as an administrator, he was known as the most economical studio head in the business, apart from Disney. Never forgetting the terrible struggle the studio had before it gave birth to talkies in the late 1920s, Warner insisted on every picture being made on the tightest budgets, and the director who overran them could expect fireworks. Anyone who rejected an assignment would be suspended. Bette Davis was told by Humphrey Bogart that if she had any more suspensions "you'd be the San Francisco bridge." Warner and his production chief, Steve Trilling, in close consultation with the writers, put the elements of a picture together in advance, cast it, then hired the director to come in at the end and handle it. Irving Rapper would be best for women's stories, Vincent Sherman for melodrama, Michael Curtiz for films calling for massive action. Cameramen had orders to keep the shadows dark and heavy or fogthick, so as to conceal the cheap sets Warner used. Away from the studio—known as San Quentin by its hard-driven employees—Warner was a splendid host, giving lavish parties, which were surpassed only by those of William and Edith Mayer Goetz. He was glowingly cheerful, cut from the same cloth as Douglas Fairbanks or Errol Flynn.

At 20th Century-Fox, Nicholas' brother Joseph Schenck, a stylish, shady extrovert who had married a film star (Norma Talmadge) and served a term in jail (income tax evasion), was nominally in charge. But actually the studio was run by two very different men: the bearlike, guttural Greek, Spyros Skouras, was head of the studio in New York, with the small, thin, buck-toothed, intensely creative Darryl F. Zanuck in charge of production on the West Coast.

Both these men shared a gambler's instinct, incredible drive, and immense personal charm; both were usually in accord on major points of policy and had made the studio synonymous with luxurious sets, glamorous women, stories of romance and high adventure, all more or less in the Schenck/Mayer tradition.

At Columbia, Harry ("White Fang") Cohn was the head of a studio that had none of the immense resources of Metro, Warners, and Fox. At Universal, a group of nonentities ran the studio until late 1946, replaced in that year by the polished, pleasant, mild-mannered William Goetz, a former associate of Darryl F. Zanuck at 20th Century-Fox who had since formed his own company, International Pictures, which he merged with Universal to create handsome productions like *Ivy* and *Temptation*. RKO was under the guidance of Floyd Odlum, the cool multi-millionaire head of the giant investment and financing corporation, Atlas. Odlum had saved the studio from bankruptcy in the 1930s, and controlled the studio's policy of tasteful, well-upholstered films. His production head in 1946 was N. Peter Rathvon, a businessman with whom he had been associated for many years and whose chief skill lay in giving an unusual degree of responsibility to his producers. Republic was run by the bullish, outgoing Herbert J. Yates and his wife and chief star, Vera Hruba Ralston, a former Czech ice-skating champion ("She skated out of Czechoslovakia into the hearts of the American public" was one famous slogan for her). Outside of the studios were the men with their own independent units: the heads of United Artists, for instance, or the civilized David O. Selznick and the aggressive, malapropish Samuel Goldwyn.

In 1946, all of these men felt reasonably secure about their future and that of the industry as a whole. True, there had been an eight-month studio strike in 1945, resulting in a 25 percent pay rise in 1946, and there seemed some doubt about the public's continued interest in musicals: *Yolanda and the Thief,* a Metro film starring Fred Astaire, normally a box office favorite, had not done very well; nor had some from other studios. But that cloud was only a tiny one on the horizon. Was there nothing ahead but happiness?

3

The answers were swift and sure in coming. Within a year,
serious omens darkened the sky. In August, 1947, Britain's
Chancellor of the Exchequer, Hugh Dalton, following a
severe postwar dollar shortage, announced that in future
75 percent of all American film company earnings in the
United Kingdom would be heavily taxed. Schenck, Louis
B. Mayer, Skouras and Zanuck, Jack Warner and the other
industry leaders sat in a series of anxious, scotch- and cigar-
laden conferences, reminding the knowing that, far from
being in competition, the film studios were as subtly inter-
connected as banks or airlines. Led by a decision of Schenck's,
the moguls panicked—a not uncommon reaction—and decided to stop the flow of films to Britain entirely. They gambled on the British public, starved for escapist fare after
months on austerity rations, demanding the return of highly
colored Hollywood fantasies to their screens. But nothing

happened, and a few months later the Hollywood moguls, humbled (comparatively speaking), began shipping limited amounts of Ann Sheridan or Greer Garson across the Atlantic.

The temporary loss of Hollywood's biggest export market upset 1946's golden applecart. The talk was loud and nervous at Chasen's, the Brown Derby, and Romanoff's, and the studio commissaries had the air of Wall Street drinking bars after the 1929 crash. An 8 percent drop in theater attendance that fall gave further cause for alarm, and exhibitors began complaining as loudly as New York critics that Hollywood stories were too slick, empty, and superficial to please war-hardened audiences.

The definite and increasing loss of public interest in escapist, glossy American films as a whole was occasioned not merely by the effects of the G.I. Bill and the local lecture courses taken by housewives on the home front. It was due to the rapid increase in the cost of living; the need to dig in and start a solid family life, arrange mortgages, buy family cars, raise children or put adolescents through college. Bobby-soxers and their college dates still necked in the balconies, of course, and the sales of pop corn and bubble gum to some extent soothed ruffled Hollywood brows. But the masses of people over thirty began, long before the television boom, to desert the movies, discovering a variety of other diversions: bowling, for one, or a revival of the thirties craze for miniature golf, and the pressure of pitiless postwar advertising to buy bigger and better everything.

In September, 1947, Louis B. Mayer cut his MGM staff by 25 percent, Harry Cohn following suit by reducing his own by 33⅓ percent. Cost-cutting became obligatory: Frank Capra slashed half a million dollars from the budget of his Katharine Hepburn–Spencer Tracy political comedy *State of the Union* by eliminating seventeen days of shooting; Preston Sturges carved his schedule on *Unfaithfully Yours* by forty-three days and saved one-third of an overall $3 million budget. There was a return to the kind of cheaply made gangster picture popular in the thirties: Hume Cronyn sadistically commanded a jail in *Brute Force,* Victor Mature and Richard Conte fought it out as cop and robber in *Cry of the City,* and Richard Widmark sniggered psychotically in *Kiss of Death.* Made in hard, stark blacks and whites, these pictures temporarily restored critical and popular faith in Hollywood.

In 1947, the structure of the industry remained monolithic. In New York, banks like the Chase Manhattan, closely linked with the studios since the Depression when heavy loans became necessary to save the companies from ruin, still put up massive amounts on the basis of a magic name like Skouras.

Banking involvement had been almost exclusively Californian in the silent period, with the Bank of America— inspired by the enthusiasm of its founders, the Giannini Brothers—supplying most of the finance on a handshaking basis. In 1929, though, after talkies came in and enormous new sums were needed for conversion of theaters and studio stages, the move east had begun. That year, the Chase Manhattan Bank (among others) moved into the industry and assumed great power.

The Chase Securities Corporation formed a syndicate with two lesser partners to issue debentures of Fox Film Corporation stock to the tune of $30 million. The Depression wiped out all hope of selling the debentures and in fact the Chase Securities Corporation collapsed largely because of its involvement in Hollywood. The bank was left with undigested assets in the form of film and theater debts amounting to $83 million in Fox Film, Fox Theaters and General Theaters. After a dogged process of recapitalization, Chase wound up with one-third of the stock of General Theaters, 58 percent of the stock of Fox Theaters and one-third of the stock of Fox Film Corporation. The Chase reorganized—brilliantly, as it turned out—Fox Theaters into the National Theater Corporation, of which it owned 58 percent again in stocks.

In 1933, Darryl Zanuck, appointed to Fox after a first-class career at Warners, achieved with William Goetz an unbelievable twelve winning pictures out of fourteen. Francis Ross, executive vice-president of the Chase Manhattan, told me in 1970, "We bought out Darryl and Billy and took a long-term contract with Zanuck. . . . Fox Films became 20th Century-Fox, a name we approved.

"We had eliminated most of their debts by converting the company, as we were entitled under the law, into stock which was then sold to the public. Over twelve years we were able to get back $85 million. But we never really lent Fox any money.

"Along about 1936, 1937, and 1938, some of the other New York banks started to get a little hungry and thought they could make some easy money in the film industry. I never lent a nickel. Some of these banks got burned because they were dealing with something they didn't know about. My guess is that the California banks did well because they were on the scene."

By 1946, the film banking situation was very much an involvement based on deep investments in the 1929 period, followed by increasing power, as companies collapsed in the thirties, and a partnership achieved by ingenious reconstruction of the companies. A major film company's name was sufficient to ensure a giant corporate loan—and in those days there were still bankable stars and even directors, magic names that could be bandied across a conference table or over lunch between men like Francis Ross and Darryl Zanuck. But no one even then believed in the automatic success of any star, best-selling property, or a Hitchcock or Lang. The only thing then, as now, a bank was interested in was the promise of a "major" to distribute, the word of an industry leader that every effort would be made to promote a film successfully, and last and most important, that every cent of the debt plus interest was repayable from the film company's other proven assets in real estate or oil.

The big companies' salesmen, chosen for their smooth ability to talk to anyone and to gear their responses and remarks precisely to the inflections of a personality, traveled the country enforcing exhibitors to buy pictures in blocks. If a man wanted to show a Greer Garson or Humphrey Bogart picture he would have to buy a string of second-grade works designed only to "keep the presses busy," not because the films had any particular merit on their own. These included specialized curios, works made by "independents" (with Bank of America money loaned on guarantee of distribution by a major) and the vast mass of B-pictures, as well as personal A-budget indulgences of men like Mayer or Zanuck.

Because of the block-booking situation, practically any film could be sold in 1947, sure of getting at least its cost back on a minimum guarantee. Sometimes unfortunate exhibitors had to buy productions not only sight unseen, but unmade as well, and still at the pipedream or preliminary treatment stage. In addition, an unmerciful war was waged against the exhibitor. In some towns the majors owned so many theaters that it was impossible for an independent to procure anything worth showing at all. Schenck and the other moguls liked to feel they owned not only the entertainment but the audience as well, and woe betide anyone who tried to take that precious public away.

Block-booking practices had not gone unobserved. Since the thirties, a constant battle had been waged by the American Government to break the situation down. As early as 1933, a beleaguered group of product-less independents had plucked up courage to take a drastic and daring step. Seizing on a month when Hollywood was in particularly low spirits after a slump in business following the first fine flush of the newly fledged talkies, the tiny Victoria Amusement Company of Camden, New Jersey, decided to take up arms against Warners, which had for years exercised raw power in the area. On January 16, 1933, the company's owners filed a petition in the Camden Federal District Court seeking the dissolution of what they termed "a motion picture trust," which sought to "impair and destroy" the business not only of the Victoria Amusement Company itself but of all independents in the area, thereby violating the Sherman Anti-Trust Act of 1890, which forbade restraint of trade and monopolistic practices.

Fifty-two celebrated attorneys representing the Hollywood and Camden opposing interests arrived in town on January 20 and filled the largest hotel. At the Camden Federal District Court, the local judge examined two piles of documents three feet high. Understandably, the case became so complex that it was rapidly dropped. But the Camden group achieved its purpose: it excited the interest of the FBI, which was sufficiently impressed to begin a full-scale investigation into the industry's theater activities.

For five years federal agents went into cities and towns across the nation finding out what Hollywood was up to. They checked carefully on how many theaters were in fact owned by the great studios in particular areas, how they exercised power by preventing others from obtaining first-run products, and the methods they used to damage the business of their competitors (which included introducing agitators into local unions and increasing fees for projectionists and ushers so heavily that no independent could afford to hire them). In Hollywood itself, FBI men obtained files and ledgers, interrogated film sales managers, and talked to studio chiefs. Then, five and a half years afterward (on July 20, 1938), the Department of Justice included its mountain of evidence in a suit naming Loew's–MGM, Paramount,

(23)

Radio–Keith–Orpheum, Warner Brothers Pictures, 20th Century-Fox Corporation and (though they owned not a single theater), Mary Pickford, Douglas Fairbanks, and Charlie Chaplin of United Artists as guilty of "monopolistic practices and gross violations of the Sherman Act."

Will Hays, the ferrety former Postmaster General whose role as head of the Motion Picture Producers' and Distributors' Association made him the industry's self-appointed arbiter, was asked by the industry's leaders to intercede with President Roosevelt. Accompanied by attorneys for the majors, he arrived at the White House on July 25, 1938.

In his tiresome Indiana twang Hays shrilly addressed a bored and impatient Roosevelt. He argued that the Anti-Trust Act needed revision in view of Hollywood's production–distribution pattern, which would be "wrecked at a blow" by any severance of the theater outlets from their owners. He described the Department of Justice's suit as "legalistic" and said that competition between theaters owned by the majors and the small groups was "healthy and fair." Roosevelt listened to him, then turned his flagging attention to the attorneys, who promised him they would "self-regulate the industry's business practices" if the government would "ease off."

The language of a Chicago crime ring combined with the self-serving content of a defensive Hollywood so rattled Roosevelt that after his guests had departed he personally issued a statement denying the validity of his visitors' arguments. He, in his whole New Deal philosophy and in the policies that sprang from it, was utterly opposed to strength of the kind Hollywood exercised. He refused a second proposed visit by Will Hays, and impatiently referred the entire matter back to Attorney General Cummings.

It was in March, 1939, that a dismaying figure emerged to quash any hopes Hollywood might have nourished of an early settlement: Thurman Arnold was appointed Assistant

Attorney General in charge of the Anti-Trust Division.

Arnold was in every way an extraordinary personality. Known as "the number one trust-buster of the nation," and as "a cross between Voltaire and a cowboy," he was a vigorous extrovert in his late forties, a wholehearted New Dealer with a hatred for combines and cartels equal to Roosevelt's own. His free-flowing, bawdy, Rabelaisian speech had been heard through the bleating lambs of his Midwestern ranch; in the foothills of the Rockies where he had homesteaded; and in heated, colorful Yale debates. He had even been the vociferous mayor of Laramie, Wyoming, a figure as carved-rock American as Will Rogers or Gary Cooper. His books, *The Folklore of Capitalism, The Symbols of Government* and *The Bottlenecks of Business,* somehow contrived to make a mockery of big business as well as subtly succeeding in upholding the native ideals of free enterprise and open competition. But his fierce hatred of monopolies was on every page.

Hollywood presented a heaven-sent opportunity for the publicity-hungry Arnold to step firmly into the spotlight only a short time after he has assumed office as Assistant in Charge of Anti-Trust Cases in March, 1939. As well as Hollywood, the building trade had his harsh attention. By May, 1940, he had succeeded in getting seventy-four indictments against eleven cities, involving as many as 985 indicted individuals.

When the Hollywood delegation returned to Washington in late 1938 and again in 1939, Arnold made it clear that its employers' activities would be treated in the fashion they deserved. Finally, as aggravated by Will Hays as Roosevelt had been, Arnold told Hays flatly, "Unless your people are stripped of their theaters it will be a public scandal." He referred his vistors back to a statement made in January, 1936, by Federal Judge George A. Welsh, who said that "refusal to furnish first-run films to exhibitors amounts to a trade conspiracy."

On June 3, 1940, the Department of Justice's suit was finally brought before New York Federal Court Judge Henry W. Goddard. Pointing dramatically at the now characteristically massive heap of FBI evidence on the polished oak table before him, Arnold delivered one of his typical opening addresses—vibrant, energetic, and full of vivid Wyoming turns of phrase. He closed with an extraordinary burst of eloquence, reminding the court of the conditions of the Sherman Act, "to prevent the growing organization of the machine age from destroying industrial democracy." He pointed out that "political democracy dies when industrial democracy dies."

The Hollywood attorneys had one night to chew over that. Next morning, Thomas D. Thacher, attorney for Paramount Pictures, opened the case for the defense. In a speech that sounded rather like the work of an anxious West Coast publicity department, he puffed the sheer excellence of the distribution system. "Paramount," he said, "has progressed in the extraordinary perfection of its product, in the amazing service of its distribution, and in the excellence of conditions surrounding its exhibition." He added that the industry had in fact fought monopolistic practices when, in the past, the Motion Picture Patents Company and the General Film Company had tried to take over the industry.

Arnold heard him out, then replied, "The danger in this country is the private seizure of power. It is subject to no checks and balances, it is subject to no elections every four years, it is subject to no criticism and no attacks because no one even knows about it.

"It is private seizure of power which the Sherman Act prevents. If we are to maintain an industrial democracy we must stop the private seizure of power and that is exactly what we have in the film industry." Next came his most deadly shaft. He informed the court that the only reason his Department was not pressing criminal charges against Louis

B. Mayer and Jack Warner and their colleagues was that previous governments had neglected to charge them and that "it seems a little late to start."

That statement provoked the most formidable of Hollywood's attorneys into a speech as heated as Arnold's own. John W. Davis, who represented MGM, carried with him Louis B. Mayer's and Nicholas Schenck's highest hopes of success. The Presidential candidate beaten by Coolidge in 1924, he had retained, the Metro lions believed, enormous personal prestige in Washington. Unfortunately, their faith was misplaced since Davis's aggressive speeches, as violent as his muckraking election deliveries of the twenties, simply aggravated Arnold and Judge Goddard. Contemptuously shaking a fist at Arnold, Davis brought smiles from his confreres as he called the Wyoming cowboy "a knight in shining armor."

The wranglings continued for days. Finally, Arnold, some felt unwisely, suddenly and unexpectedly began to make a compromise deal. He entered into an arrangement with the attorneys whereby the film companies would cease—after a period—forcing theaters to take films they did not want, and that they would immediately agree to stop harassing and penalizing independents. In return for this promise, Arnold agreed to let the majors temporarily retain the chains of theaters themselves—the whole question of the severance to be suspended for three years. A special Arbitration Commission was set up to ensure that the matter was kept under scrutiny.

During the three-year period between 1940 and 1943, the film companies' attorneys constantly tried to seek an extension of the time allowed, determined to wriggle from under the Sword of Damocles and hoping against hope that the entire matter would be dropped. They at least succeeded in outstaying the reign of Thurman Arnold, who became a judge. On October 8, 1945, the whole matter was finally reopened, with Attorney General Francis Biddle (short-lived because he never really got along with President Truman) in charge. Biddle appointed Robert L. Wright, his special assistant, to handle the case.

The morning the hearing opened—five years later and again held at the Federal Court in New York—John W. Davis stormed in holding his brief like a shield and, barely waiting to hear Robert Wright's opening address, harangued the three judges, Henry W. Goddard, John M. Bright, and Augustus N. Hand. Again using the kind of language familiar on the twenties hustings, he shouted intemperately, "This action is a hobbyhorse by which the government expects to find a cure-all for the many ills of the industry." Ralph Harris, attorney for 20th Century-Fox, added a no less unfortunate observation when he said, "I have never heard even the government claim it could regiment our society into a Utopia." These statements, to say the least, made a poor impression. Wright was greatly relieved when Colonel William Donovan (representing RKO) admitted he had nothing to say, since his colleagues had said it "more than eloquently" for him.

Three weeks later, the hearings, marked by more vivid displays of temper from John W. Davis and some sharply worded speeches by Robert L. Wright, were still dragging on. That day, Adolph Zukor, creator and head of Paramount Pictures, and then past seventy, denied the monopolistic practices with which he had been charged; he was the only movie mogul to risk the unblinking eye of the court judges. Toward the end of the hearing, Wright said that "the defendants control about 65 percent of all pictures produced from the selection of the story to the final showing in the theater," suggesting that this in itself constituted monopolistic practice and that Hollywood might be a healthier place if it were made up of small independents.

Wright produced evidence of illegal minimum ticket price

"fixing" and pinned up a number of charts showing cities that were excessively dominated by the studio chains. Whitney North Seymour, representing Paramount on this occasion, said that "any court action would stifle Paramount's ability to compete." Davis added in a plea for mercy that "there is a common feeling of sympathy among the defendants because this disaster has descended on them," but he infuriated the other attorneys by calling for "justice for Loew's alone." He said that the current situation held "no serious menace" for the industry, and that "long experience has shown that the producer–owner circuits work out better than the independent units . . . largely because the independents do not have the vision or the capital to promote themselves to the fullest advantage." He unfortunately had missed the fact, as Wright later made clear, that the reason they did not have capital was that the studios were preventing them from obtaining it.

Much to the delight of Davis and his fellow attorneys, the three judges were far from satisfied by Wright's pile of 362 separate items of evidence, ruling sixty-two of them "totally irrelevant." The case was twice adjourned while Wright was called on to produce more effective materials. (He showed FBI records that the defendants owned three hundred theaters in five hundred towns.) Still reprieved from selling their theaters, the companies were required to stop all minimum admission price agreements, any techniques for stopping competitive business, and all formula deals or master agreements with theater groups. From July 1, 1947, no exhibitor would be penalized by being handed second features because he did not belong to a major chain, and he would not have unwanted features forced upon him.

There it seemed the matter would rest, with Hollywood still, despite a series of compromises, many of which it cheerfully ignored, in charge of its distribution machinery. But yet another colorful—and publicity-conscious—figure emerged to shatter the industry's hopes: the new Attorney General, Tom Clark.

Clark, who enjoyed, and relished, the title of "General" when it was addressed to him, was a massive, ten-gallon-hatted Texan, then in his late forties. His aggressive legal background, garish range of bow ties, and his long, quizzical nose earned him a constant flow of attention from the nation's press. When he took up the reins at the Department of Justice, he attacked his job with an energy even Thurman Arnold might have envied, announcing from the first that he would devote all of his energy to exposing and destroying the monopolies.

Like Arnold, he was perfectly conscious of the value of making the film industry a prime target. Intensely annoyed by the court's compromise decision, he had the entire case reopened and refought through the lower courts in 1948. Price fixing, block-booking, pooling agreements—all these were already prohibited, and no further defensive action could be taken even by the most zealous Hollywood companies. But the one single action Clark was bent on was to wrest, once and for all, every last theater from the majors.

In Hollywood, news that the whole matter had been raised again—that the compromises agreed to had not been effective in saving the moguls' imperiled skins—caused a new wave of conferences which resulted in the company attorneys, led by John W. Davis, preparing an ingenious system of "consent decrees" designed to save endlessly expensive litigation in the years to come.

Some hoped—and Howard Hughes, now owner of RKO-Radio Pictures, even daringly proposed—that it would be possible for shareholders to sit on the boards of both the theater and film-making organizations after the splits occurred. The "consent decrees" (to sever voluntarily exhibition from production–distribution) would, some believed, not actually damage the structure of the industry. But Clark saw

(30)

through that ploy right away, and Hughes' scheme for RKO was summarily rejected.

Ironically, as Clark proceeded to press for the consent decrees to be entered into, which he himself found satisfactory and time-saving arrangements provided they were adhered to faultlessly, he found that a number of other companies (among them the Griffith Amusement Co. and three other Texas, Oklahoma, and New Mexico chains) were acting in breach of the Sherman Act; several of these had been among the most determined fighters of the majors' ownership themselves. Upon reinspection, the Supreme Court rejected an earlier compromise measure: that independent theaters should enter into competitive bidding for product.

A series of decisions against Hollywood, followed by the implementing of the consent decrees under a special new Board of Arbitration designed to put them into effect, came as a severe blow to Mayer, Warner, and the rest, as well as to men like John W. Davis. Legally speaking, and in terms of strict idealism, the government's action, doggedly pursued by men of the caliber of Thurman Arnold and his successors all the way up to Tom Clark, was perfectly sound and was a desirable result of Rooseveltian liberal thinking finally achieved after seventeen enormously costly and difficult years of investigation and petitioning. But in practical terms the victory of the Department of Justice and the independents over wicked Hollywood had incalculably disastrous effects on the film industry and the very character of film entertainment itself. For confidence in a product, the feeling that it could flow out along guaranteed lines of distribution, was what gave many Hollywood films before 1948 their superb attack and vigor. Also, the block-booking custom, evil though it may have been, ensured that many obscure, personal, and fascinating movies could be made and released, feather-bedded by the system and underwritten by more conventional ventures. Arnold, Wright, and Clark may have scored a victory for justice, but they scored a defeat for entertainment, and in effect struck Hollywood—except Paramount, which had found its 1,800 theaters a burden in the matter of overheads—a blow from which it has never recovered.

The years 1947–1950 brought another death blow: the political witch hunt which stripped Hollywood of even a middlebrow intellectual confidence for more than a decade.

4

The roots of Hollywood's political troubles lay deep in its very earliest history. Self-made and poorly educated, Schenck and certain of the other moguls grew up with the attitude that unions could be silenced by bribes to their leaders, that intellectuals were to be mistrusted or emasculated by money, and that there was something threateningly "leftist" about a good many of them. Until the mid-thirties, the political attitude of certain Hollywood figures was so crude and makeshift in its near-fascism it was scarcely possible to take it seriously. True, the labor conditions of Hollywood had resulted in important strikes, most notably at the dawn of the talkie era, when, caught off guard by public taste, the industry's leaders drove their workers like Paraguayan miners to make movies on 18- to 20-hour or even 24-hour shifts. But neither the workers nor the bosses had even the beginnings of a cohesive political position, merely echoing faintly the protests and corruptions of the more sophisticated east.

It was in 1934 that the political scene in Hollywood began to focus for the rest of the country. The elections for a new governor in that year were contested by the Republican Frank Merriam and the muckraking intellectual Democrat, novelist Upton Sinclair. Sinclair was a strong opponent of Hollywood's business methods, a Left Wing thinker *par excellence*. It was entirely predictable that William Randolph Hearst, along with Louis B. Mayer, should marshal his massive funds behind Merriam. Employees of various studios were informed that they must not make the mistake of supporting Sinclair and were asked for a day's wages to swell the campaign coffers.

According to Leo Rosten's *Hollywood: The Movie Colony, the Movie Makers* and Bosley Crowther's *Hollywood Rajah*, MGM manufactured fake newsreels, with extras dressed as anarchists and other riffraff, crossing the border to assume control of Hollywood if Sinclair were elected. One of these sequences was drawn from an actual movie, *Wild Boys of the Road*. After a bitter campaign marked by such excesses, Sinclair was defeated.

The Merriam election infuriated Hollywood's more New Deal-oriented people, who by forming the Motion Picture Democratic Committee in 1938 succeeded in pushing a Democratic candidate—Culbert Olson—into power. In the meantime, the high feelings that split the Hollywood community on the Republican–Democrat issue were intensified by a still more momentous clash between the American Legion at one extreme and a group of special factions—Communists, pro-Nazi Fascists and Bundists—at the other.

It was only a step from baiting the Democrats to baiting those further to the Left. By a process of self-deception, many industry Right-wingers, including Nicholas Schenck and Harry Cohn, succeeded in working their way into an almost pro-Hitler position, castigating the Left-wingers for the Communist anti-Nazi position. The Hollywood Anti-Nazi League had among its members many prominent directors, writers, and players of an anti-establishment persuasion. It was all too easy to use the inflammatory word "Communist" to describe them all.

Meanwhile, in Washington an organized body had been quietly formed to combat communism within the United States. In May, 1938, Martin Dies, Texas Representative of the Democratic Party in Congress, set up the House of Representatives' Committee on Un-American Activities, designed to flush out subversives of every dubious political color as well as to further Dies' flourishing political career. A lanky, drawling, roughly humorous lawyer with no liking for intellectuals, Dies was cast in the same mold as the Hollywood moguls themselves, with their small-town European mentality shifted bodily to suburban Los Angeles.

Despite the fact that he started his Hollywood inquiries in 1939 on altogether the wrong foot—damning several Hollywood stars for sending greetings to the Left Wing Paris paper *Ce Soir* including absurdly the eleven-year-old Shirley Temple—he received a warm welcome there. He spent that year collecting evidence through FBI agents and others, determining that fifty anti-Nazis were certainly heinous Communists, a theory he maintained even after the signing of the Hitler–Stalin pact. In all his investigations he was enthusiastically backed by Buron Fitts, the Los Angeles District Attorney who had decided to run for re-election on an anti-Communist platform.

For both men, a cleaning out of the Hollywood backyards was clearly an opportunity to win fame and prestige among the vast masses of Conservative Americans. Every statement Dies or Fitts made won front-page space, and they were particularly quotable when in August, 1940, they made it clear that Hollywood Communists were connected not merely with subversion but with murder.

Fitts issued a statement to the Los Angeles press that after

(35)

several years of investigations he had determined the instigators of a 1935 murder of John Riley, a San Pedro harbor merchant seaman. The instigators were, he said, members of a Communist ring; one of whom, a longshoreman named Brittain Webster, was undoubtedly guilty of the killing and was immediately arrested for it. Then came the first of the carefully compiled Fitts/Dies lists: among those named as members of the ring, but not actually accused as parties to murder, were the actor Lionel Stander (whose recent performance as a movie agent in *A Star Is Born* had been warmly praised), a little-known director named Herbert Biberman (*One Way Ticket, Meet Nero Wolfe*), and his wife, the well-known actress Gale Sondergaard, the playwright Clifford Odets, and Samuel Ornitz, writer of the screenplay of *Imitation of Life* and *The Return of the Vampire*. Dies immediately subpoenaed them to appear before him at a small committee hearing in Los Angeles. Receiving his subpoena, Ornitz said, "I have murdered people—but only in the movies."

The subpoenas were served on August 4, 1940. On August 5, the former executive secretary of the California Communist Party John Leech made an extraordinary statement to the grand jury at the hearing on the Riley murder. Already outspoken in his denunciations of Hollywood's involvement with Communist activities, he now rattled off an astonishing *Who's Who in Hollywood* list of eighteen Hollywood "Communists" including Fredric March, Humphrey Bogart, Franchot Tone, James Cagney, and Francis Lederer, most of whom had sinned only in the sense that they had supported anti-Nazi meetings.

Leech was patently a worthless witness, branded by Dean James Landis of the Harvard Law School, who had had him as a student, as "an almost pathological liar." Many people thought that Fitts, acting with the aid of Hollywood moguls who had for more than a decade supported him in office, had simply used Leech as a mouthpiece for his own prepared charges.

On August 16, Dies held the first of his all-star hearings in a Los Angeles hotel. Humphrey Bogart, furious and accompanied by a battery of television and film cameras, told Dies and his fellow committeemen, Robert E. Stripling and James Stedman, that the charges made by Leech were "without foundation, absurd and ridiculous." Soon after that, Leech released more names, bringing the total to forty-three.

As the Dies hearing continued throughout August, Dies' family received threats of murder. Pricked by these threats, Dies launched into a new series of public statements, saying that many Hollywood actors were guilty of working with Russia. The Screen Actors' Guild replied vigorously, saying, "The members . . . hate Nazism, Communism and fifth columnists, whom America must smash. To smear prominent persons without reliable evidence is to play into the hands of Hitler and Stalin by confusing the innocent with the guilty. . . . Such are the tactics which have been resorted to by fifth columnists everywhere." Simultaneously, Y. Frank Freeman, president of the Producers' Association, demanded a full-scale continuation of the investigation (scarcely necessary in the circumstances) in order to improve the "presently tarnished" public's view of the industry's 32,000 employees.

After several weeks' work, Dies was forced to admit he had failed to discover one shred of evidence that would suggest subversive activities in Hollywood. It became obvious, in fact, that the Communist Party in California, as in the rest of the country, was weak and fragmented; that the signing of the Hitler–Stalin pact destroyed at a blow the anti-Nazi position for which isolationists had criticized the Left Wing; and that it forced many of the more idealistic members of the Party into an emasculated neutralist position revised only when Hitler made war on Russia.

During World War II, the Un-American Committee occupied itself mainly with flushing out fascism at home, and communism—especially after America entered the war with Russia as an ally—was left largely unharassed. In 1945, a half-hearted attempt was made by the Committee to start a new investigation, but it was hurriedly dropped. The atmosphere of the Cold War however gave the Committee another opportunity to investigate. Inspired by a speech made by Winston Churchill at Fulton, Missouri, in 1946, President Truman issued an order demanding a loyalty oath from all government employees, swearing they were not members of the Communist Party. It was the beginning of a wave of mass hysteria as Communists started to be flushed from under every bed, and mere affiliation with Left Wing groups was considered sufficient to result in firings, demotions, or outright persecution.

It was true, of course, that the threat of espionage existed, and that whole areas of internal security were threatened by Communist spy rings, as the trials of the Rosenbergs, Alger Hiss, and Judy Coplon later successfully proved. Yet the hysteria was insane, nonetheless. It lay in accusing innocent and patriotic members of the Party of attempting to aid in the overthrow of the government. The charge became, as it had been in 1940, ludicrous in the case of Hollywood actors—few of them more than rudimentarily sophisticated in a political sense—and desperately ironical in the case of writers for motion pictures, all of them plying their typewriters in the service of studio heads with specific aims in mind. Yet, as in 1940, the Committee saw an ideal opportunity for publicity in Hollywood, gleefully preferring activity there instead of in book publishing, the theater, religion, or education, all of which had their periods of investigation later on.

Head of the Committee in 1947 was a tiny, red-necked, overwrought insurance broker named J. Parnell Thomas (he had altered his name from Feeney in his youth because Thomas rang out more resoundingly than his own). In an atmosphere of Cold War his small, intense hatred flourished like an underwater plant. He had been at one time a member of the Dies Committee, and he had long envied his master's fame. Late in 1946, Thomas announced that on taking charge of the Committee in January, 1947 (it came under Republican control after a period under the Democrats, on January 3), he would "expose and ferret out" Communist sympathizers in Hollywood. In California the hysteria grew almost hourly. In 1946 the *Hollywood Reporter* began an anti-Communist campaign which was capped by reprinting an article from *The American Photo-Engraver,* written by Matthew Woll, naming various actors as Communist sympathizers. Among those named were Myrna Loy and Orson Welles, both of whom reacted by lodging million-dollar damage suits— Miss Loy against the *Reporter,* and Welles against Matthew Woll. In October, 1946, the California Legislature's Committee on Un-American Activities (independent of the Washington Committee), subpoenaed the president of the Screen Writers' Guild, Emmet Lavery, who said correctly, "there are probably Communists in Hollywood, but they have no opportunity to get their doctrine into motion pictures." Similarly subpoenaed, Byron Price, chairman of the Motion Picture Producers' Association, not unwisely remarked that "E. J. Mannix, Y. Frank Freeman, and Louis B. Mayer"— studio chiefs all—"are not Communists."

As in 1940, the names of the accused grew starrier as their listing increased. Edward G. Robinson, Burgess Meredith, and J. Edward Bromberg were interrogated, as well as those listed in 1940 (James Cagney and Lionel Stander among them). In a public statement defending his article in September, Matthew Woll said he was horrified that Myrna Loy should have supported the American Slav Congress, a pro-Tito organization, that Edward G. Robinson should have supported the Conference on China and the Far East, as well as the American Youth for Democracy, "which pledges its members to fight against the United States in the event of war with Russia." By an engaging irony, only a month before—in August—Ilya Ehrenburg in Moscow accused American producers of "stamping out free thought" in their movies.

In March, 1947, Eric Johnston, president of the Motion Picture Association of America, told the House Committee that he was satisfied Communists were not "significantly influential" in Hollywood. A month later, statements by various political figures were becoming more hysterical. Los Angeles City Councilman Ed J. Davenport told a meeting of the American Defense League at the Hollywood Roosevelt Hotel that the Communists locally were being supported by an "eastern gambling syndicate." Hedda Hopper added her husky, raucous voice to the general hubbub. In her column, syndicated across the country, she indicated that Hollywood films had often been pro-Soviet (in view of the fact that Russia was America's World War II ally, what else they could have been is far from clear). *"Mission to Moscow,"* she wrote, "distorted history; *North Star* showed a Russia which never existed; *Song of Russia* a musical [*sic*], seemed to prove that the Russian industry was based on a five-year plan devoted exclusively to the production of violins."

From February on, the Committee began to hunt for evidence of pro-Communist propaganda in wartime and postwar scripts. On March 2, a mass meeting of 3,000 was held at Los Angeles Philharmonic Auditorium when on the platform Mrs. Lela (mother of Ginger) Rogers and State Senator Jack Tenney bitterly attacked Emmet Lavery and actor Albert (*Dr. Cyclops*) Dekker, who had also taken up the defense of the Hollywood Communists, largely on the ground that they were harmless.

On May 15, J. Parnell Thomas and his Committee members established their headquarters at the Biltmore Hotel in Los Angeles, beginning their activities by questioning Mrs. Rogers, Paramount production executive Harry Ginsberg, Richard Arlen, Robert Taylor, the *Esquire* magazine critic Jack Moffitt, and Roy Brewer, spokesman for the International Alliance of Theatrical Stage Employees. Robert Taylor told Thomas that he had been prevented from entering the Navy until 1943 in order that he might appear in *Song of Russia*. Thomas enthusiastically announced, "*Song of Russia* was Communist propaganda that favored Russia, its ideologies, its institutions and its way of life over the same things in America." Moffitt unhesitatingly laid the guilt for Hollywood communism at the door of Broadway, which had spawned so many of its writers.

First to be singled out for blame by those concerned were that embattled group of intellectuals, the writers. Mostly playwrights and novelists without large reputations, lured to the California sun by offers of large sums of money (the very best could earn $100,000 a picture), they had little or no opportunities to infiltrate a single fragment of personal viewpoint, let alone "Communist propaganda" into their movies. Most had grown up in the thirties, when intellectuals had rallied almost en masse to the Marxist cause. Many were anti-Stalinist and opposed to an internal revolution in their country. Yet their "longhair" qualities, at once encouraged and emasculated by the producers earlier on, now brought out a Philistinism and—if they were foreign—xenophobia in the moguls and their minions that had, if truth be told, never been far from the surface.

Screenplays were more often than not drawn from the works of others, either slavishly followed or seriously compromised, and approved, checked, and filtered by a battery of executives from the head of the studio down. Expensive hacks, trying to redeem unsuitable novels or plays with their gruelling assignments, the writers were during the war years forced to produce the crassest propaganda films, patriotically desirable but artistically worthless. Among these were such figures as John Howard Lawson, Ring Lardner, Jr., Albert

Maltz, and Herbert Biberman—all destined to become notorious in the months that followed Thomas's appointment.

Still less capable than the writers of introducing ideas, Communist or otherwise, into the entertainments of forties Hollywood were the actors or even the directors, who were largely under long-term contract and handed assignments the refusal of which could mean instant suspension. If anyone was guilty of infiltration of ideology it was the head of a studio himself, since he with his advisers propelled projects into production and engaged staffs to carry them out.

From the first moment that Thomas moved into the Biltmore, the studio bosses realized they had to escape any possible charge of using their studios for pro-Communist purposes, even though in the pro-Soviet atmosphere of World War II they had produced pictures idealizing life in the Soviet Union and glorifying anti-Nazi communes in countries shortly to be locked behind the Iron Curtain. Desperate to escape the atmosphere of public suspicion that then reigned and whipped up by the media to a point of intense fear against Communists, the moguls one by one began to condemn their own former employee–writers who had worked on pro-Soviet propaganda, pretending they had fired them when in fact they had not and asserting that they had removed lines critical of monarchy or presidency from important scripts.

By this action, by their fear and by their later introduction of the blacklist, the industry chiefs in fact helped to wreck their own business in the year to come. Just as they had aggravated the Department of Justice into precipitate action in 1947 by fighting the severance of the theater chains in an unbecoming fashion through intemperate attorneys and by squirming for escape and constant harassment for delays in judgment, so in the same fatal year they turned on their own employees and colleagues, wrecking at a blow Hollywood prestige in Europe, the confidence of the Hollywood intelligentsia, and all chance the industry might have had to keep up with the revolution in mass education that followed World War II. When they met at the Waldorf-Astoria that winter to prepare a document banning all Communists or suspected Communists from future employ, they barely dented the growing Communist front of the time. They only struck, firmly and furiously, a whole series of nails in their own coffins.

The charges made within and without the industry of Communist propaganda became more ludicrous as the May hearings wore on. John Howard Lawson, a noted Left Wing critic and historian, was shown to be iniquitous because he had scripted *Action in the North Atlantic,* a hymn to the American Merchant Marine which idealized the comradely life of sailors and showed the humble, noble efforts of ordinary Americans to bring a relief convoy to Murmansk. Imprecations were heaped on the authors of Sam Goldwyn's *The North Star,* full of starved peasants and gnarled elders fighting with hoe and fork the enemies of Russia. The film featured such peasants as Anne Baxter and Walter Huston, trying to look Slavic. *Song of Russia* earned anger for its authors too. It was a simple-minded story in which an American orchestra conductor (Robert Taylor) conducted bowdlerized MGM versions of Tchaikovsky from one end to the other of hammer-and-sickledom. Also attacked was Jack Warner's *Mission to Moscow,* a lavish propaganda work as carefully made as it was historically suspect.

At the May hearings, the novelist Ayn Rand announced her intense dislike of *Song of Russia.* Mrs. Lela Rogers said she had deterred her famous daughter from making a version of Theodore Dreiser's *Sister Carrie* since it was "open propaganda"—cheerfully ignoring the fact that it had been written more than four decades before its author became a Communist. She also denounced *Tender Comrade,* which Ginger had actually appeared in, because it showed girls in wartime

(43)

sharing and sharing alike, and *None But the Lonely Heart*. This last film was scripted by Clifford Odets, and starred Cary Grant as a lower-class Englishman who would become the Unknown Soldier of World War II.

Director Sam Wood was equally determined to ferret out imaginary wickedness. Adolphe Menjou, Morrie Ryskind, Fred Niblo, Jr., Robert Montgomery, Ronald Reagan, Gary Cooper, Leo McCarey, Walt Disney, Jack Warner, and Louis B. Mayer all added their pinches of spice to an already heady mixture of blame, praise, reassurance, and condemnation. Their testimony filled the days until the June departure of the Thomas Committee for Washington.

Ahead lay the Waldorf summit meeting of the studio chiefs, the serving of subpoenas to nineteen writers and directors, and the taking by ten of them of the First Admendment to protect their colleagues and force their prosecutors to put them on trial. It was to be the blackest of periods in the history of Hollywood, with results more fatal to film content than could be calculated in the years to come.

5

During the summer and fall of 1947, FBI agents were not merely busy flushing out particulars of Hollywood's heinous theater-owning practices, they were unearthing more serious details—the activities of the film community's known Communists and Communist sympathizers. Among those they pursued, ten were destined to become world famous in the months that followed, earning a notoriety their Hollywood slave labor had notably failed to achieve. Two of the group were in the $100,000-a-year class, at the top of the Hollywood heap: Dalton Trumbo, formerly a novelist *(Johnny Got His Gun)*, more recently the scenarist of two Ginger Rogers vehicles, *Kitty Foyle* (which won her an Oscar) and *Tender Comrade,* and John Howard Lawson, author of scripts for *Action in the North Atlantic* and *Sahara.* Albert Maltz, though wasted on screenplays for mediocre films at Paramount and Warners *(This Gun for Hire, Cloak and Dag-*

ger), undoubtedly possessed the most formidable intelligence of the group, and today emerges as its most impressive member. He had had an interesting prewar career as a New York dramatist. The others made up a mixed bag: Edward Dmytryk, director of the anti-anti-Semite film *Crossfire,* and his producer Adrian Scott; writers Alvah Bessie, Lester Cole, and Ring Lardner, Jr., author of the witty script for George Stevens' *Woman of the Year;* Herbert Biberman, and the late Samuel Ornitz. None, save Lawson and Trumbo, was in the first rank of Hollywood professionals; none was an outstanding creative artist. It was another special irony that their careers would barely have attracted the attention of serious critics on both sides of the Atlantic if it had not been for their appearances before the Un-American Activities Committee.

All strictly patriotic, they had—it is now clear—no intention whatever of using the films they worked on as vehicles of subversive propaganda. Lawson may have glorified the convoys that relieved Murmansk in *Action in the North Atlantic,* but he was acting properly in a propagandist function at a time of the American alliance with Russia. Cole may, in *Song of Russia,* have sinned equally, but again he acted in the interests of his bosses, who quickly fed him to the wolves. Those were harrowing times, and the hysteria fed by the first inquiries of the Thomas Committee reached a high peak by the time of its first official Washington hearings in mid-October.

Held in the Caucus Chambers of the Old House Office Building, the hearings were staged with all the flair of a Cecil B. DeMille spectacular. From two massive chandeliers, klieg lights hung in clusters, providing a dazzle of illumination for the batteries of newsreel cameras. Four hundred spectators jammed the brown leather seats, witnesses were led to a polished table bristling with microphones and flanked by whirring cameras on tripods, while around them, squatting, standing, or sitting on the floor were packs of reporters scribbling away in shorthand the testimonies of the famous.

J. Parnell Thomas carefully placed himself at the very center of attention: on a high dais behind a long desk like a Spanish inquisitor. Propped on a bulky, white, Washington business directory, he looked as pompously crimson and pleased with himself as a prize-winning apple. Shattering seven gavels in a row, he jumped up and down like a jack-in-the-box, hugely enjoying every second of his self-arranged fame, hectoring all save the friendliest witnesses in his harsh, cockerel's voice.

On the first day of the hearings—October 21—five hundred people fought for the limited space and a hundred were turned away. They had come to see the stars. Once inside, they looked bored by the news that nineteen people in whom they had not the slightest interest (including the Unfriendly Ten) were fighting against being called in evidence at all. Robert W. Kenny, former Attorney General of California, together with Charles Katz and Ben Margolis, an important attorney representing the accused, immediately sought from Thomas a quashing of their subpoenas on the ground that the Committee had "no constitutional power to censor political, social or economic ideas and was barred by the Constitution from inquiring into matters of thought, speech or opinion." Supporting him in this plea stood other attorneys for the nineteen, including San Francisco's Bartley Crum, author of the President's favorite book, *Behind the Silken Curtain,* and New York's Samuel Rosenwein.

Thomas glanced up to make sure the cameras hadn't missed a nuance of his facial expressions as he histrionically informed the attorneys present that their plea would be dismissed at once. Pale with anger, they sat down, and the first of the witnesses, Sam Wood, was called to the stand.

Director of *For Whom the Bell Tolls, Saratoga Trunk,* and *King's Row,* a staunch Right-winger with a stolid, unimaginative directing style, Wood was the president of a curious organization called the Motion Picture Alliance for the Preservation of American Ideals, designed to hunt down longhaired leftists of every creed and color, and a prime inviter of the Thomas Committee to Hollywood. He denounced the directors Irving Pichel, John Cromwell, Edward Dmytryk, and Frank Tuttle as "agents of a foreign power" and the three writers, John Howard Lawson, Dalton Trumbo, and Donald Ogden Stewart as men with "Communist leanings." When Robert E. Stripling asked him if he had any doubt in his mind that John Howard Lawson was a Communist, he replied—to a wave of laughter—that if there was any doubt, he did not "have a mind." He also excited the audience into prolonged amusement when he said that at a recent rally Katharine Hepburn had appeared and helped raise $87,000 for a "very special political party" which certainly "wasn't the Boy Scouts."

Next to appear was Jack Warner, natty and sunburned, swaggering to the stand as ostentatiously as a John Barrymore or an Errol Flynn. Obviously relishing the spotlight, he announced that he had not renewed the contracts of a number of writers he suspected of wanting to sneak Communist propaganda into Warner Brothers movies, among them Clifford Odets, Alvah Bessie, Ring Lardner, Jr., Albert Maltz, Dalton Trumbo, and John Howard Lawson. He said proudly that, thanks to the most scrupulous vigilance, no Communist propaganda had emerged in any of his pictures. His film *Mission to Moscow,* based on the memoirs of the former American Ambassador to Russia, Joseph E. Davies, had been made, he said, at a time when Soviet Russia was America's ally, and contained nothing subversive of America itself.

Louis B. Mayer, as diminutive as Thomas, followed Warner with a robust defense of his studio and of Hollywood as a whole. He pointed out that his much criticized film *Song of Russia* was—in common with Warner's *Mission to Moscow*

—produced at a time when the American government was encouraging urgent efforts to aid Russia, and when Russian morale was at a low point during the siege of Stalingrad. It was absurd to call the work propagandist. Repudiating Robert Taylor's statement made in Los Angeles in May that the work was subversive, he declared, "It's just a boy-girl romance featuring a Russian setting and the music of Tchaikovsky." He also pointed out that the late Frank Knox, then Secretary of the Navy, had postponed Taylor's enlistment especially to permit him to make the movie. *The Battle of Stalingrad*, Mayer said, "was after all a documentary with a prologue expressing high tribute from Mrs. Roosevelt, the Secretaries of State, War and the Navy, Generals Marshall and Mac-Arthur."

Next to be called was Ayn Rand who, as in May, denounced *Song of Russia* as "a vehicle of Communist propaganda" and did not spare *Mission to Moscow* either.

On October 22, Jack Moffitt, movie critic of *Esquire*, launched a violent attack on Hollywood as a whole, adding that Broadway, too, was dominated by communism. When he said that members of the Hollywood Story Analysts' Guild —readers who advised on whether synopsized properties should be bought—had deliberately written bad synopses of non-Communist works to squeeze through their Communist friends' work instead, attorney Charles Katz shouted, "He's naming some of my clients!" and began cross-examining Moffitt without invitation. Thomas ordered Katz thrown out of the room. Seized by a policeman, the attorney was frog-marched to an elevator and carried down to the lobby, where he was forcibly ejected into the street. Moffitt then handed a delighted Committee copies of the alleged Communist Party cards of writers Dalton Trumbo, Ring Lardner, Jr., Lester Cole, and several others, all of them in the possession of the *Hollywood Reporter*.

The most elegant of witnesses, Adolphe Menjou, arrived

sporting a brown striped suit by the leading Fifth Avenue tailor, De'Gez, a Sulka tie, and a Clark Gable shirt, speaking in elocution school English through a scrupulously curled mustache and clouds of cigarette smoke. He delivered a lengthy speech about Marxist doctrine, announced that Hollywood was "a world center of Communism," and suggested that a Communist invasion might be imminent, aided and abetted by certain stars, writers, and directors.

"If the Russians came here I'd move to Texas, because I think the Texans would kill them all on sight," he said to a room of hysterically laughing people. The atmosphere was lightened also by Paul V. MacNutt, former diplomat and counsel for the Motion Picture Producers' Association, who threw his clients to the winds with the remark that "98 percent of Hollywood motion pictures are soap—Ivory soap."

As the inquiry went on, the statements became more and more heated. Replying to assertions by Jack Warner and Louis B. Mayer that they had dismissed writers they suspected of Communist sympathies, scenarist Guy Endore said, "Warner investigated me and put me on the subversive list . . . then took me off." Clifford Odets denied Warner had dismissed him and said that the studio was currently negotiating for screen rights to two of his plays, *Clash by Night* and *Rocket to the Moon*. Writer John Wexley said he had resigned willingly from Warners in 1941, and that the only changes made in his scripts were to "save money." The Screen Directors' Guild issued a public statement flatly denying its member Sam Wood's charge that his fellow members John Cromwell, Irving Pichel, Edward Dmytryk, and Frank Tuttle were guilty of communism. William Wyler attacked Sam Wood, saying that the "only undemocratic activity" he could recall within the context of the Guild was Wood's attempt to introduce an oligarchical system for nominating members.

Writer Morrie Ryskind said, "If Lester Cole is not a Communist, I don't think Mahatma Gandhi is an Indian." Fred

Niblo, Jr., another writer, noted, "I can't prove my colleagues are Communists any more than I can prove the people massacring Custer were Indians." Asked whether his films *Going My Way* and *The Bells of St. Mary's* had been successful in Russia, Leo McCarey said, "They have a character the Russians don't like." "Bing Crosby?" "No, God."

If figures like this provoked the spectators into much mirth, then the appearance of various film stars to give testimony caused even headier excitements. The court was jammed to standing on October 23, when Robert Taylor squeezed in through a thousand fans. One middle-aged woman, dressed in a red hat, stood on a radiator to get a better view of her idol and fell flat on her face in front of the astonished Committee. The 90 percent female audience sighed as Taylor sat facing the batteries of cameras, shrieking "Hooray for Robert!" when he said, in answer to the question "Are you an actor?" "Since 1934." He announced, to a loud show of hands, that the Communist Party should be outlawed and that if he had his way they would all be sent back to Russia. Actress Karen Morley and actor Howard da Silva were two whom he branded "possible Communists." Saying that he had not wanted to appear in *Song of Russia,* he agreed with Ayn Rand's estimate of it as a "propagandist work."

Writer Howard Rushmore and MGM story department head James W. McGuinness talked of "Communist pressure" groups opposing *Gone With the Wind* and *Tennessee Johnson* because those films criticized Negroes. Ronald Reagan, tanned and handsome in a gabardine suit, caused ecstatic reactions among his fans as he delivered an eloquent speech against Communist infiltration in California, presaging his career as governor two decades later. Robert Montgomery and George Murphy admitted the presence of Communists in Hollywood, but said that they were "insignificant" and did "little harm." Gary Cooper declared that Communists in Hollywood had dared to tell him "America would be better off without a Congress," a remark that brought the house down.

Summing up their evidence at the end of October, *Newsweek* noted that the "friendly" witnesses had established that Communists in Hollywood numbered only one percent, but that they were "extremely well organized, extremely active, and extremely troublesome."

After a weekend recess on October 25–26, the Committee reconvened and announced that for the first time nineteen "unfriendly"—i.e., Communist—witnesses would be called. Planeloads of stars arrived in Washington in support of the nineteen, led by Humphrey Bogart and Lauren Bacall, and a series of lavish press receptions and cocktail parties was arranged. This group of stars and their friends became known as "The Committee for the First Amendment," because the Unfriendly Nineteen invoked the First Amendment in refusing to give evidence of their Communist affiliations before the Committee. The Nineteen's purpose was to obtain a Supreme Court ruling on the rights of a congressional committee to make a Communist identify himself.

First to be called to give evidence was John Howard Lawson. Explicitly named a Communist by the Committee——which produced what it alleged to be his Party card No. 4525—he flushed angrily as a 5,000-word history of his presumed association with various Communist front organizations was read. On cross-examination by Thomas, he clashed bitterly with him, shouting, "I am not on trial—it is the Committee which is on trial before the American public." After accusing Thomas of trying to intimidate him, Lawson, shrieking protests, was seized by six policemen and plunked down firmly in a front-row spectators' seat. Eric Johnston protested Thomas's conduct of the inquisition, but was severely reprimanded for doing so. When Robert W. Kenny, attorney for the Nineteen, again tried to have their subpoenas quashed, he was as violently ill-treated as the witnesses themselves.

During the next days, more writers were cross-examined: Dalton Trumbo, Albert Maltz, and Alvah Bessie, all of whom, like Lawson, had largely been engaged on anti-Nazi propaganda pictures during the war, not one of which had the slightest trace of Communist ideas (or, the unkind might add, of any other).

They acted vigorously, delivering personal insults with all the panache of the Committee itself, describing Thomas and another Committee member, Representative Rankin of Mississippi, as "Goebbels and Himmler." Alvah Bessie said, "The true purpose of this Committee is to provide the atmosphere and to act as the spearhead of the really un-American forces preparing a Fascist America." All refused to state whether they were or were not Communists, Maltz saying that the questioning itself was "an obvious attempt to violate my constitutional rights."

Dalton Trumbo—like Maltz and (in part) Bessie—was permitted to read a statement. His was probably the most colorful. It read: "I would rather die than be a shabby American, groveling before men whose names are Thomas and Rankin, but who now carry out activities in America like those carried out in Germany by Goebbels and Himmler.

"The American people are going to have to choose between the Bill of Rights and the Thomas Committee. They cannot have both. One or the other must be abolished in the near future." When Robert E. Stripling asked Maltz if he had been a Communist, Maltz said, "I have answered, Mr. Quisling."

There can be no question that in the heat of the moment, the Hollywood Ten, as they came to be known (nine of the nineteen were never prosecuted), acted intemperately, using the same name-naming and smearing techniques and tactics as their accusers. Each was cited for contempt of court, and each was compelled to return to California in the certain knowledge that his arrest would soon follow.

On October 30, the hearings abruptly ceased, with only

ten of the Unfriendly Nineteen actually prosecuted in person. The reasons for the cessation were various: a consolidated attack on the Committee by press, radio and television; the necessity to begin hearings immediately on a separate Howard Hughes investigation; and a threat of a full-scale Communist demonstration to be staged the day the Committee next heard witnesses. Counsel for the Ten immediately sent a request to the Speaker of the House of Representatives, Joseph W. Martin, asking him to "decline to certify for contempt of Congress the ten witnesses who were ordered from the stand by Chairman J. Parnell Thomas during the hearings last week." The statement concluded with the words "The Committee's sole purpose is to intimidate artists, writers, and directors and to compel the entire film industry to conform to the Committee's notions of what is desirable for presentation on the screen." Martin rejected the plea.

In November, the hearings apparently at an end, an all-important meeting took place at the Waldorf-Astoria in New York. Among those present were Nicholas Schenck, Barney Balaban, Eric Johnston, J. Cheever Cowdin, president of Universal Pictures, Jack and Harry Cohn, Spyros Skouras, Samuel Goldwyn, Walter Wanger, and Dore Schary, vice-president of RKO. Walking about informally—no board meeting was actually held—these industry chiefs discussed the hearings in great detail. Schenck held the floor on several occasions, pointing out that if Hollywood did not clean its nest immediately by blacklisting and firing all suspected Communists, the public would desert Hollywood films as products of a subversive community. He made it clear that the banks were strongly in support of an industry blacklist, and Eric Johnston, overruled by Schenck (who in fact had the power to dislodge him if he had proved recalcitrant), had no alternative but to renege on his precious promises and issue the fatal pronouncement which became known as the Waldorf Statement.

The Waldorf Statement read by Eric Johnston November

25 at a special press conference following the summit meeting was as follows:

Members of the Association of Motion Picture Producers deplore the action of the ten Hollywood men who have been cited for contempt by the House of Representatives. We do not desire to pre-judge their legal rights, but their actions have been a disservice to their employers and have impaired their usefulness to the industry.

We will forthwith discharge or suspend without compensation those in our employ, and we will not re-employ any of the ten until such time as he is acquitted or has purged himself of contempt and declares under oath that he is not a Communist.

On the broader issue of alleged subversive and disloyal elements in Hollywood, our members are likewise prepared to take positive action.

We will not knowingly employ a Communist or a member of any party or group which advocates the overthrow of the government of the United States by force or by any illegal or unconstitutional methods.

In pursuing this policy, we are not going to be swayed by hysteria or intimidation from any source. We are frank to recognize that such a policy involves dangers and risks. There is the danger of hurting innocent people. There is the risk of creating an atmosphere of fear. Creative work at its best cannot be carried on in an atmosphere of fear. We will guard against this danger, this risk, this fear.

To this end we will invite the Hollywood talent guilds to work with us to eliminate any subversives; to protect the innocent; and to safeguard free speech and a free screen wherever threatened.

The absence of a national policy, established by

Congress, with respect to the employment of Communists in private industry makes our task difficult. Ours is a nation of laws. We request Congress to enact legislation to assist American industry to rid itself of subversive, disloyal elements. Nothing subversive or un-American has appeared on the screen. Nor can any member of Hollywood investigations obscure the patriotic services of the 30,000 loyal Americans employed in Hollywood who have given our government invaluable aid in war and peace.

Following the statement, Dore Schary, vice-president of RKO, who had promised no severe action against employees suspected of Communist affiliations, was forced to yield to pressure in the dismissal of Adrian Scott and Edward Dmytryk, producer and director of *Crossfire*. (He later claimed to have voted against his own board when the decision was made, but a resignation would have been more effective.)

In appearance, Schary was the ideal figure for a spoof: tall and avuncular, with soft blue eyes and massive hornrims, a tweedy Walter Pidgeon version of an American highbrow, he had been honored with profiles in *The Christian Science Monitor* and *Look,* and belonged to religious organizations. He had always been known as a "liberal" film writer, more comfortable in Hollywood than most. Born in 1905, he was a haberdashery salesman, china buyer, and printer's devil before he became an actor, playing walk-ons in Broadway problem plays like *Four Walls* and *The Last Mile*. He wrote plays in his spare time; Walter Wanger discovered and encouraged him sight unseen, thinking "Dore" was a woman's name. Disappointed when he met Schary, he was too embarrassed to cold-shoulder him, and obtained him a promised contract at Columbia. Schary later worked for Metro, where he wrote glutinous films which gladdened

Mayer's heart: *Boys' Town; Young Tom Edison; Edison, The Man,* and *Journey for Margaret.* Working later for David O. Selznick, he wrote the equally sentimental *I'll Be Seeing You.* He was loaned to RKO in 1946 and produced *Till the End of Time* and *The Farmer's Daughter.* In January, 1947, he was appointed vice-president in charge of production. He made *Crossfire,* a picture about hatred of Jews in America that masqueraded as controversial despite Jewish control of Hollywood, and a sickly plea for tolerance called *The Boy with Green Hair.*

Schary's role in the Hollywood Ten matter was a very significant one. A representative of the Hollywood rank-and-file, the only "intellectual" present at the summit meeting, and the only man not a mogul, he found himself unable to protect his colleagues, due to the fact that his power was reduced by his superiors at a crucial time. His colleagues are still bitter: Adrian Scott, producer of *Crossfire,* told me, "I'll never forgive him. He promised to set a precedent, never to fire anyone because he was suspected of being a Communist. Then, as soon as things got hot, he simply let us go." Four days after the Waldorf conference, Schary received the Golden Slipper Club's 1947 Humanitarian Award.

Ironically, only six months after that conference, Schary was forced to resign from RKO anyway. When Howard Hughes took over the studio in the spring of 1948, he canceled Schary's patriotic war film *Battleground* and three other projects, leaving the way clear for Schary to resign. Immediately Louis B. Mayer and Nicholas Schenck hired Schary—pleased at his role in the Hollywood Ten inquiry and convinced he would bring a policy of reasonably priced but thoroughly respectable films to Metro. It was a decision they both had cause to regret.

In August, 1948, Schary was in New York for a press conference, at the same time consulting with Schenck on his production plans. He told Seymour Peck, then of the New York

Star, today head of *The New York Times* Sunday "Arts and Leisure" section, "I will make daring and controversial pictures for MGM. They haven't been making any lately." Peck asked him what pictures answering that description MGM might possibly have made in the past. "Oh, *Mutiny on the Bounty,*" Schary said, mentioning his own films *Joe Smith American, Journey for Margaret, Pilot No. Five,* and *The War Against Mrs. Hadley,* as well. "Were these controversial?" Peck asked. "They tried to create an understanding of the war. We will make respectable films for a respectable world . . . in which intolerance, hate, and venality are dispensed with. They say we don't produce adult pictures. What are adult pictures—adultery? We have no use for such subjects. I don't think art is four-letter words written on bathroom walls."

Peck pinned him down to a question of the Hollywood Ten. "Would you," Peck asked, "fly in the face of your recent statements and hire a Communist?" "If I were confronted with proof that a person was affiliated with an organization designed to overthrow the government I would not employ him at Metro." Peck wanted more. "Will men like Adrian Scott and Edward Dmytryk work again soon?" Schary hedged. "As you know, there are court cases going on about that [so] I'd rather not comment. I can't predict anything." Would *Schary* employ them, Peck persisted. "The industry adopted a policy about them when they said they would not be employed until they had purged themselves of contempt proceedings. It's an *industry* policy."

In the wake of the Waldorf Statement, it became obvious that the witch hunt had served no useful purpose at all, and in fact had divided an industry already threatened by the theater-chain battle in Washington and innumerable other problems. The investigation had failed to produce evidence of Communist propaganda in motion pictures, a fact to which J. Parnell Thomas astonishingly confessed in an article in

Liberty Magazine in June, 1948: "I have since realized that my idea was both ambitious and dangerous [and that] motion picture criticism should not be a function of Congress." His confession was more disingenuous than it seemed. He was in fact annoyed that he had not tried to prove instead that the Unfriendly Ten were part of a vast Communist plot to take over the film industry—a plot which, if it existed at all, was only a dream expressed at some of the more hot-headed Communist meetings in Hollywood.

In May, John Howard Lawson and Dalton Trumbo were sentenced to $1,000 fines and one year in jail by the Washington District Court. The intention was to appeal to the Supreme Court, where the majority of judges were thought at the time to be favorable to the Ten. The remaining eight witnesses waived the right to jury trial. Many of the jurors at Trumbo's and Lawson's case were government employees —all save one in Lawson's instance. "That one was a woman, and when she came back on the 'guilty' verdict, I saw she was crying," he says today.

In New York, all members of Actors' Equity had to sign written pledges of non-Communist affiliations. Darryl F. Zanuck rushed out 20th Century-Fox's *The Iron Curtain,* a ludicrous parody of a Canadian Russian spy case, shot on Ottawa locations. Warners came in with another propaganda piece, *To the Victor,* and MGM with *The Red Danube*— all designed to show that Hollywood's heart was in the right place, and at the same time losing it limitless prestige in Europe.

Not long after the Waldorf Statement, Dore Schary appeared before the Screen Writers' Guild, with Walter Wanger and Edward Mannix of MGM, to explain the decision to the assembled members. He immediately stated his dislike of the conclusions of the Waldorf meeting, and the purposes of the Producers' Association as follows: The Ten unfriendly witnesses would most definitely be fired, no one known to be a Communist would be employed, and a justification campaign would be launched to aid Hollywood's image. In return, Schary implied, no further prosecutions would be made and the remaining nine of the Nineteen would be spared. On December 5, the Ten were indicted by a senatorial majority on a charge of contempt of Congress, and five days later they were placed in custody of the U.S. Marshal in Los Angeles.

A series of suits was lodged against the major companies— by Lester Cole and Dalton Trumbo against MGM, and by Edward Dmytryk against RKO among others. (After four years of litigation, the sued companies settled out of court for $107,500 damages.)

At a meeting in New York, Gerhart Eisler, called the "brains" of the American Communist Party, and Eugene Dennis, Party secretary-treasurer, met with four hundred incensed people, seven of the Hollywood Nineteen, and, among those sympathetic to the Ten, Humphrey Bogart, Lauren Bacall, Lon McAllister, Evelyn Keyes, June Havoc, Paul Henreid, Jane Wyatt, and fifteen other stars to condemn the Committee's supposedly fascist character. Ex-Assistant Attorney General Thurman Arnold and Governor Herbert Lehman of New York were among the protesters, Arnold calling the Committee investigation "an inquisition of the motion picture industry which violates the First Amendment." That night, CBS broadcast a radio skit in which Groucho Marx played Chairman Thomas haranguing witnesses.

For two years, the Unfriendly Ten fought to have their case heard in the Supreme Court. They firmly blame the death of two friendly judges—Wylie and Rutledge—on the fact that the Court finally declined to sit in judgment on their case at all. Whatever the reason, they were never heard, and a series of civil actions in the lower courts resulted in the firm upholding of their sentences.

On June 8, 1950, John Howard Lawson and Dalton Trumbo, handcuffed together, were driven to the District of Columbia jail in Washington by United States marshals. Earlier, a thousand demonstrators in New York had marched in protest against the writers' imprisonment.

Trumbo flew in from Los Angeles and was met by Lawson at La Guardia Airport. Trumbo told reporters, "We are angry and resentful at having to go to jail. But I don't see how we can do otherwise in all conscience."

On June 19, on the eve of their own trial in Washington, seven of the Ten (Adrian Scott, the eighth, was in a hospital in Hollywood) had appeared at a meeting in the New York Town Hall, sponsored by the National Council of the Arts, Sciences and Professions, at which 1,250 people petitioned President Truman to stop the trial and pardon Lawson and Trumbo. Louis Untermeyer told the crowd that the defendants were "on their way to a great destiny. . . . They stand for the creation and preservation of what they and I think of as our American culture." From England, Bernard Shaw sent a message denouncing "an abominable persecution," while Paul Robeson closed the hearing with a group-sing "to escort the Ten to their honorable imprisonment."

The Ten served sentences in different parts of the country. Lester Cole and Ring Lardner, Jr., at the pleasantest of these—Danbury, Connecticut—drew agreeable consolation for their plight by finding among their fellow inmates none other than the irascible J. Parnell Thomas himself.

In November, 1949, Helen Campbell, a gray-haired spinster in Thomas's employ, had sobbingly confessed to Washington officials that her boss had been stealing money from the government. He had for years been paying $20,000 a year in salaries charged up against Congress to a group of women—including Helen Campbell's relatives and Parnell Thomas's aunt and daughter-in-law—not one of whom had in fact done any more than hand over their salaries to him.

The columnist Drew Pearson, who for months had been pressing charges against Thomas, pushed still harder for justice. An embarrassed government was forced to dislodge Thomas from his role as witch baiter and in late 1950, after futilely invoking the Fifth Amendment, he was packed off to Danbury with a thirty-two-year sentence (virtually death to a man over sixty) and a fine of $40,000.

Before Thomas's parole (Truman later mysteriously granted him a free pardon—one of the last of his acts as President), Lester Cole passed the furious man working on the chicken coops. "Still cleaning up chicken shit I see," Cole said.

With the Ten firmly in jail in different parts of the country, and Thomas behind bars at Danbury with two of them, it was obvious that all Thomas had succeeded in proving was that mere membership in the Communist Party was sufficient to justify a jail sentence if you wouldn't confess to it.

In the wake of Thomas's arrest, the Committee advisedly relaxed its attack on Hollywood. But not for long. In 1950, a "third wave" of witch hunting began; however, John Wood, Democratic representative for Georgia who replaced Thomas, was as impotent as his Republican predecessor in proving that anything subversive had occurred.

In some ways, Wood's inquiries were even more savage than Thomas's, though they were not as publicly ballyhooed. Immense new lists of names were drawn up. Sterling Hayden revealed that he had once been a Party member but had left it in 1946; Larry Parks, chain-smoking and near tears, admitted membership between 1944 and 1945 and dramatically informed on a number of his colleagues after saying he would not do so; John Wayne called on the industry to "forgive" Parks, but Hedda Hopper furiously denounced Wayne for his action and he was forced to withdraw the suggestion next day.

Most vigorous of the new wave of 1950–1951 persecutors was Victor Reisel, syndicated columnist for the Post-Hall Newspaper group. At a meeting of more than a thousand people at the Hollywood American Legion Auditorium, he announced peremptorily that the Hollywood film industry was being "exploited by the Communists. . . . The film industry knows who the Communists are," he said. "Unless it puts a stop to them by mid-April, the industry will receive one of the worst black eyes it ever received. The members of the Communist Party were lined up with Hitler when he gassed 60,000 Jews. So don't let the Commies ridicule you by calling you anti-Semitic. Where were Larry Parks, Gale Sondergaard, and Howard da Silva when we let them know that slave labor was just managing to exist in Russia on seven hundred calories a day? They were standing at the edge of a swimming pool singing 'Arise ye prisoners of Starva tion.' "

Hedda Hopper wrote in her column in March, 1951, "I feel impelled to speak the minds of the mothers of the 55,000 casualties in Korea. I have sympathy for anyone who sees the light. But Mr. and Mrs. Larry Parks were visited by the FBI four years ago. The FBI pleaded with them to get out of the Communist Party. They threw him out of the house. I believe the life of one soldier fighting for our freedom is worth all the careers in Hollywood. . . . I am wondering if the mothers and families of those who died will be happy to know that their money at the box office will continue to support those who have been so late in the defense of our country."

When Paul Jarrico—author of *Thousands Cheer* and co-author with Lester Cole of *Song of Russia*—was served with a subpoena reporters asked whether he would comment on Larry Parks. "If I have to choose between crawling in the mud with Larry Parks or going to jail with my courageous friends of the Hollywood Ten, I shall certainly choose the latter," he said. Gale Sondergaard admitted to *The New York Times* (March 25, 1951) "I would be naïve if I did not recognize that here is a danger that . . . I may have reached the end of my career as a motion picture actress."

Howard da Silva, who had played the barman in *The Lost Weekend,* angrily denounced the Committee. Will Geer, Victor Killian, Fred Graf, Waldo Salt, John Garfield, Anne Revere, Jose Ferrer, and dozens of others were interrogated. By far the most sensational confession came in April, 1951, when Edward Dmytryk, after his jail term, admitted that he had been a Communist all along. He spoke of "well-intentioned citizens being caught in Communist flytraps," and that communism had sought control of all Hollywood's guilds and craft unions. The purpose, he said, was to infiltrate Communist propaganda into motion pictures, and he named as other Communist members of the Screen Directors' Guild in 1945, Frank Tuttle, Herbert Biberman, John Berry, Bernard Vorhaus, Jules Dassin, and Michael Gordon. Dmytryk made clear that the membership of the Communist Party at that time involved "no menace" and that the spy trials of the Rosenbergs, Alger Hiss, and Judy Coplon and the Korean War had changed his mind.

Others joined the accused: Karen Morley, Fred Rinaldo, Lew Solomon, Michael Uris, Georgia Backus, Hugo Butler, Leonardo Bercovici, Ed Huebsch. Parks was dismissed from his starring role in a picture called *Small World* at Columbia on the grounds that "Columbia cannot foretell how long Parks will be tied up in Washington." Betty Garrett, wife of Parks, collapsed on hearing that her husband had confessed he was a former Communist. "This will wash me up in Hollywood," Parks told the Los Angeles *Examiner* (March 23, 1951). He was right: He never worked in Hollywood again.

It was the start of a progressive ruining of hundreds of Hollywood employees, and the end of intellectual content in

Hollywood for more than a decade. The Ten and their fellow Communist sympathizers had a severe, widely publicized struggle for restitution of their right to work. Herbert Biberman boldly went out and made a pro-Communist film, *Salt of the Earth*, at Silver City, New Mexico, in 1953, in collaboration with International Union of Mine, Mill and Smelter Workers. Paul Jarrico, one of the spared last nine of the Nineteen, worked as his assistant. Ring Lardner, Jr., and Adrian Scott went to England and worked largely in TV under assumed names. Others went to Mexico: Dalton Trumbo—reconstituted with much well-planted publicity by Otto Preminger, who hired him as writer of *Exodus*—even won an Oscar for *The Brave One* under the assumed name of "Robert Rich," a cause of exquisite embarrassment to the industry chiefs. Many of the Ten are unemployed today. John Howard Lawson believes the blacklist still operates against him. But Albert Maltz has returned strongly with his screenplay for *Two Mules for Sister Sarah* and work on *The Beguiled*, and Ring Lardner, Jr., has had an enormous *succès d'estime* with M*A*S*H.

In the last analysis, all the Thomas and Wood witch hunts proved was that Hollywood screenwriters were pathetically unable to impose any intellectual or ideological content on their scripts, and that writers were generally regarded in Hollywood as the lowliest of bank clerks or counter-hops. It might be claimed, perhaps even with some justice, that the talent swept out of the door by the witch hunts was unimportant. Yet in the wake of that period, not even the most mild Left Wing or even liberal thinker could infiltrate an idea of any kind into Hollywood films. And that was the tragedy.

6

Shorn of most of its ideas and many of its talents, stripped of its theaters, Hollywood in the early fifties faced another threat to its existence: television. With increased problems of automobile parking in overcrowded cities, and the pressure on the pocket of that generation's growing families, television's appeal was immense—the most addictive entertainment since the dawn of movies. And when sets became more readily available to the general pocket, the landslide was devastating. It was Hollywood's failure to meet that problem properly, to make a satisfactory marriage with the two rival television empires of NBC and CBS, that ensured its further ruin.

Television's history had been a straggling one, beginning with experiments as far back as the nineteenth century. In America before World War II, possession of a set had been restricted to the privileged few, who paid large sums to see little more than jumpy newscasts, rambling vaudeville shows, and an occasional live theatrical production. In 1939, the Federal Communications Commission firmly prevented the development of television as a major industry for six years, predicting with the prescience of an H. G. Wells what the future might bring. "We must beware," read a report made in that year, "of developments in television that might prove disastrous to the motion picture industry." Other reasons for the suspension of the rapidly increasing new manufacture were the poverty of visual quality, and the extreme crudity of the content. But CBS and NBC and DuMont spent the war period fighting a battle of their own for the development of the medium.

Contrary to report, one motion picture company as early as 1938 foresaw the possibilities of television. Paramount, very much in the forefront of talkies when all the other companies save Warners had hung back, entered the field that year when the pioneer Allen Balcom DuMont had to raise capital for a TV broadcasting station. He exchanged 56,000 shares of DuMont stock for $56,000 which Paramount supplied. The result was DuMont's WABD, foremost in its efforts to eliminate television's many maddening faults. The move proved exceedingly fruitful: by 1949, Paramount's stock in DuMont had soared to a value of $7,650,000; and it later reached approximately $10 million and more.

No other motion picture company had the foresight to realize what television might become—Schenck refused the chance to invest in NBC—and even Paramount restricted its involvement to the role of inactive or even silent partner, eschewing like every other outfit in Hollywood actual production on the spot. In 1946, the FCC lifted its restrictions, and TV sets began to be manufactured in substantial quantities. The boom was on. By 1949 a million receivers had been sold, and by 1951 ten million. "Prophets of television," wrote *The Saturday Evening Post* in 1946, "see the new medium putting a stadium, amusement park, theater and university into every home. They forecast a modern home built around the television room. Interior decorators have already designed furniture to arrange the family in concentric half-circles in front of the television screen."

Many Jeremiahs at the time were ready to predict the worst for television. They remembered the occasion when the William Morris Agency staged a variety act on television in 1926; the act ended when the television machinery brought down the stage of a specially hired theater under its weight. In the thirties, David Sarnoff's RCA managed to bring out a satisfactory tube, but sets often induced acute eye trouble, with flickering, triple images, and raging blizzards of interference.

By 1946, television still was a somewhat primitive medium. In those days—a *Saturday Evening Post* survey revealed—commercials were closely linked with an actual drama or comedy. A drama's kitchen scene involved lengthy discussion of a particular brand of kitchenware, followed by a villain falling to the stroke of an especially recommendable carving knife; if a blonde stripped to her underwear in a sexually charged sequence, the audience would see a closeup of the brand name. Cars driven by the hero were apt to be those manufactured by the sponsor—cars driven by the villain were the work of his rival.

Often, the heat on TV production sets was unendurable: a girl carrying a silver tray in a coffee commercial dropped it with a scream because it became so intensely hot; leading men sweated so violently their bronze makeup ran down their pallid cheeks. Color television demonstrations were disasters, as the contemporary critic Alva Johnston wrote: "Red objects generally televise as white. A Carmen wearing a red sash danced against a white background in the studio. On the receiving sets the red sash appeared white as the background, so that the dance appeared to be performed by a figure sawed in two."

Most shows were feebieminded affairs, ranging from cookery lessons to games for presumed adults. Telecasts were restricted to the hours between 5 and 10 P.M., with an average of thirty viewing hours a week. By 1946, new experiments began to suggest that television might survive its depressing drawbacks. The inhabitants of Newburgh, New York, used as guinea pigs for television shows since 1939, began to note improvements on their weekly answer cards, and crowds for showings in bars and restaurants improved; a series of test demonstrations in Gimbels store in Philadelphia, begun in 1945, proved increasingly popular. From a central control booth deep within the store, telecasts of commercials were flashed to twenty separate receivers scattered over the various floors. As a result of polls, customers set the pattern for the commercial-producing industry in the years that followed: an overwhelming majority voted for very short commercials, running two minutes at most. The Philadelphia shoppers also provided a guide to the presentation of a product. By the time a proper presentation had worked out, 82 percent could next day name the product shown, 22 percent said they would buy it, and 8 percent bought it within twenty-four hours. The power of television to advertise was, by December, 1946, established beyond question.

Success followed success. In the fall of 1947, RCA's new image orthicon pickup tube was marketed; a hundred times more sensitive than any predecessor, it could even record clearly the most dimly candlelit dramatic scenes. Sixteen-millimeter versions of old movies—by 1947 a staple television standby—looked excellent, and a *Citizen Kane* would no longer resemble a *Great Train Robbery* in terms of visual quality. Airplanes and airports began to feature television demonstrations, planes used televisor boards to make running checks of available space, and new horn-shaped antennas sprouted from buildings to pick up the feeblest signals.

There were problems that year, admittedly. Chief of these was a battle between various interested bodies on a crucial issue: Should television broadcasts be in black-and-white or color? Color, obviously, was depressingly mediocre, and offered severe distortion; the FCC evidently bore this in mind when, after fourteen weeks of deliberation and test demonstrations, it ruled out color for the time being in March, 1947. The battle had resolved itself into a duel of the giants: NBC was in favor of black-and-white, CBS in favor of color. NBC under RCA had $100,000,000 invested in black-and-white, and pointed out that black-and-white sets would be useless if color TV became the norm; CBS pointed out that color gave the public a more specialized entertainment quality, that audience research showed color to be preferred by the average person. Unfortunately, though, color was overruled, and perhaps unwisely the FCC did not decide in favor of alternative systems for both rival companies.

In 1945, the Army-Navy game was flashed from Philadelphia to New York. In February, 1946, the new 225-mile coaxial cable began transmissions from Washington, D.C., to New York. A group of enthusiastic watchers in New York's RCA Building could make out, at the imminent risk of eyestrain, General Dwight D. Eisenhower in Washington laying a wreath at the foot of the Lincoln Memorial. TV jargon began to emerge in the early spring of 1946. NBC issued a booklet full of unfamiliar phrases such as "womp" for a sudden flare of light across the screen, "broads" for banks of fluorescent lights, or "noodle" for a few vamped bars of background music.

January, 1947, was a red-letter month: the opening of the Eightieth Congress was shown on New York screens, provoking *Time* magazine to remark: "In this memorable broadcast, television proved that its window on history was almost as clear as a newsreel's, and far closer in time." But the same publication noted that the public really hadn't yet snapped up the new medium. "Unless television gets a move on, few in the U.S. will see a political or any other kind of broadcast by 1948."

By far the most important event of the 1946–1947 television period in terms of popularity was the Louis-Conn fight, captured by five cameras and carried by radio linkup to Philadelphia and Washington via the new transmission tower of the Empire State Building (*Life* magazine sent a cameraman up the tower to photograph a vertiginous bird's-eye view). *The New Yorker* reported in its "Talk of the Town" column (June 29, 1946) the fulfillment of a "dream of longest standing," namely "sitting on the receiving end of a television program." Its writer had seen a telecast of the Louis-Conn bout at the Knife and Fork Grill on the corner of Bleeker Street and Broadway. Looking at the Knife and Fork's battered twenty-inch second-hand receiver, the crowd of two hundred standees and seventy seated people murmured excitedly as the image flickered graying-green and the two warring giants appeared to battle in the ring; even though they often disappeared entirely, and most of the fine points of the fight were lost, the cheers and applause were deafening. Thereafter, television in bars and restaurants became overwhelmingly popular.

By 1948, television had gotten into its awkward stride. Variety shows had begun to emerge, led by such stalwarts of the legitimate stage as Edgar Bergen, whose debut was unhappily a disaster. On NBC on November 17, 1946, he appeared with his ventriloquist dolls, Charlie McCarthy, Mortimer Snerd, and Effie Clinker, and his wife, Frances Westerman. The reviews were really lethal. "He floundered vaguely in the unfamiliarity of a television set," *Newsweek* sharply remarked. But Bergen gradually improved, and Milton Berle, an early rival, emerged as the unquestioned King of Television, a comedian who adapted his nightclub style to the confines of the TV screen with effortless skill.

By 1949, television was an obsession: streets were deserted as families huddled around the shrine every Tuesday night, watching the grinning "Uncle Miltie" go through his familiar paces. If you couldn't go home or had no home to go to, if

(*71*)

the family ritual was denied you and you were a lonely city man, you could still go compulsively to a neighborhood bar and watch Berle on an eight-inch set with the other customers. Uncle Miltie's only serious rival was Ernie Kovacs, a more gifted comedian with a maniacally unpredictable streak, who, when he finally learned that his show had been canceled because of the competition from Berle, dressed up as a nineteenth-century villain in pitch black and set fire to the studio set with sinister hollow laughter, obviously enjoying the experience. Raymond Burr as Perry Mason was almost equally addictive: his slow, purring, well-fed-cat delivery, as he solved endless cases with the aid of William (son of Hedda) Hopper and the sisterly, benign Barbara Hale, was adored by countless millions. The film companies tried to answer with drive-in theaters, accompanied by pop corn and pizza, the pressure to eat relentlessly applied by attendants, but drive-ins did not really supply an answer to the monster in the corner.

In 1947, television marked time, improving sharply in 1948 with the filming of the Republican and Democratic conventions; the Republican convention, in particular, was superbly presented by NBC. "Radio, clearly, has a back seat now," *Time* magazine remarked as it noted the details of the Philadelphia gathering: Robert Taft, bespectacled, scholarly, and witty, Thomas Dewey less "couth," primitive makeup turning the smoothest chin so dark it looked unshaven, a girl delegate stifling a yawn during a dull speech, a wide-eyed little boy in the spectators' gallery. The telecast, for all its technical shortcomings, successfully captured the pressure, the razzle-dazzle, the ballyhoo of the event. *Time* wrote (July 5, 1948), "The TV camera had the run of the city; it peered and probed everywhere; and its watery gaze was somewhat unflattering. Good-looking women turned into witches and dapper men into bums. Under TV's merciless, closeup stare, the demagogue and players to the gallery did not always succeed in looking like statesmen." At one stroke, the enormous immediacy of television was established, its power to make or break a public figure by exposing his virtues and weaknesses like a spiritual X ray. And it was seen to outstrip radio and the cinema as a conveyer of reality, a mirror of life itself.

Between 1948 and 1950 television swept ahead, with one thousand new sets installed every twenty-four hours—watching the box became obligatory, a family occasion beyond compare. People started to say that television would replace newspapers, a rumor that provoked *The New York Times* in September, 1948, into conducting a survey of its own news items, determining that it ran over two thousand stories during five weekdays, a service no television outfit could hope to compete with. Other newspapers were less sanguine, and magazines began adding new and attractive features to recapture readers television was taking away. Book publishing had a period of panic, and even sporting attendances began to fall off.

It was in these last years of the 1940s that television began to have quality. Because of its victory in the FCC color vs. black-and-white battle, NBC was easily in the lead, developing—along with Paramount—a system of recording television programs on film and projecting them on movie screens in Paramount theaters. NBC and its parent RCA also worked with Warners and 20th Century-Fox on closed circuit television. Twentieth-Century-Fox made extensive theater television experiments, MGM obtained an interest in Los Angeles television stations, and RKO's N. Peter Rathvon plunged his studio into TV investments.

By 1949, the sponsors' list had quadrupled from 1946, and an average of $10 million was spent on advertising. Ford was early into the field with its baseball games; Gillette, American Tobacco, and General Foods rushed in as other major sponsors. *Fortune* reported a massive 1948 deal between 20th Century-Fox and R. J. Reynolds Tobacco: the deal was for a five-day-a-week television version of Fox Movietone News on NBC at a cost to Reynolds of $350,000 for the film and $300,000 for station charges. Gillette obtained the rights to the Louis-Walcott fight for $100,000. For a total cost of $700,000 the Yankees', Giants', and Dodgers' home baseball games were sponsored. In 1946, only 6,500 sets had been manufactured, in 1947 scarcely more than that, with the majority going into public places, but in the first three months of 1948, chiefly due to the announced coverage of the Presidential election, 279,000 were sold. *Televisor* magazine determined that in March of that year New York had 127,000 sets, Philadelphia 22,000, Los Angeles 15,000, and those figures tripled by 1950.

NBC's pioneer station, New York's WNBT, provided programs of increasing quality during the boom period. The glorious, half-forgotten era of live television began. The Theater Guild, the Kraft Television Theatre, the American National Theatre, and superb concert programs achieved something television now fails to do: they brought the best of the stage and music to the masses. Those might be the days of Howdy Doody, a tedious puppet with a line of relentless, comedian's banter, but they were also the days in which great Broadway stars could be seen by many people who would have been uneasy about going into a theater, and Toscanini conducted in your living room.

By 1951, an improvement in the TV image had encouraged some Hollywood figures to buck their contracts and make forays on the box. Claudette Colbert helped lift the taboo in 1951, when she appeared on the Jack Benny Show insisting on only one key light, putting three dresses over one arm and driving over to CBS as casually as she might set off to a weekend hotel.

Gradually, the medium's technical faults were ironed out, so that a crack made by Hollywood's establishment via the successful 1950 comedy *All About Eve* already sounded rather hollow. Marilyn Monroe, as a casting-couch hopeful, asks her protector George Sanders whether she should abandon her stage career for a television audition. "Television is nothing but auditions, my dear," Sanders says. And many movies showed someone switching on a set only to see a miserably flickering image.

Television's golden era, which immediately and startlingly followed its period of semi-amateurish struggle, is symbolized by an issue of *Time* on February 13, 1950, listing the week's attractions: *The Royal Family,* with Margaret Wycherly as the aged matriarch of a Barrymore-like theater clan; Ezio Pinza, Madeleine Carroll, and Linda Darnell in *Goodbye Again;* Marlene Dietrich in *Murder Strikes Twice;* Ethel Barrymore in *April 25th as Usual,* and George S. Kaufman, Clifton Fadiman, and Abe Burrows in a panel show, *This Is Show Business.* The Theatre Guild on the Air offered such civilized pleasures as Shakespeare productions—beginning with *Coriolanus*—and Gertrude Lawrence in Kurt Weill's *Lady in the Dark.* The Kraft Television Theatre reached an audience of millions, mingling Wilde with Wilder and Shakespeare with Tennessee Williams, while Worthington Miner's Studio One offered an extraordinary production of Turgenev's *Smoke,* a modern-dress *Julius Caesar,* and a spectacular *Battleship Bismarck.*

The New York Times' Thomas F. Brady wrote (May 2, 1948): "It is significant that, while the government is seeking to destroy distributor control of the theatrical outlet for motion pictures, the major Hollywood companies are gradually, but nonetheless purposefully, acquiring television interests." Monogram began selling a solid backpile of films to CBS, and a number of film-makers, led by the brilliant designer William Cameron Menzies and Hamilton-Whitney Productions, began making pictures for TV. The pioneer Jerry Fairbanks in 1948–1950 established a system of making

(75)

series of half-hour films for television, employing multiple camera setups, and presaging the half-hour-long episode of television shows later on. Stanley Kramer in *The Motion Picture Herald* for December 2, 1950, was quoted as saying, "Who knows? In five years we may be turning out television films."

By October, 1950, television had begun to solve the major unemployment problem of Hollywood. For the first nine months of the year, 5,660 speaking parts were filled by Screen Actors Guild members. Film producer Gordon Levoy, Gene Autry, and Bing Crosby (Fireside Theatre) all started to pour out Hollywood films for TV in 1950. Samuel Goldwyn was among those to see the giant potentialities of the medium. "The big problem which faces television is programming. . . . Only Hollywood is geared to supply that visual entertainment demand." Admissions to theaters fell off by about four million, but it was not until the three subsequent years (1950–53) that the public really showed it was drifting to home viewing. It only gradually emerged that the audience for motion pictures had fallen 20 percent since the war.

Despite the fact that Hollywood attempted a comfortable merger with television in those crucial years, its central error lay in failing to present its then contracted stars in major, planned series—in fact in banning them from television altogether. When KTTV in the fall of 1950 showed an old film strip featuring Mickey Rooney and Walter Pidgeon, their studio (MGM), led by Schenck, bitterly complained. And it became obvious at the tail end of 1950 that despite its determined efforts to marry the rival medium, the enormous power of CBS and NBC seriously threatened the industry's ability to produce, while the audience itself more and more clearly showed its preference for staying at home and enjoying its entertainment free of charge.

MGM and the other majors also refused to permit their productions to be shown on television channels—an ideal, guaranteed outlet after the failure of the battle to retain the theater chains. Humphrey Bogart expressed a general note of caution when he told the Los Angeles *Times* (August 13, 1950): "Television is a hungry monster. It will voraciously devour plays, pictures, talent, everything that it can capture. Its appetite is enormous. The individual can save himself only by proceeding carefully." Most of the moguls did not even pursue a similar wait-and-watch policy; theirs was an open (and foolish) competition—a competition that seemed strange in view of their investment behind the scenes. Hedda Hopper wrote in her syndicated column for May 31, 1950: "This is one medium that I don't believe Hollywood can give the old runaround; so we might as well take the TV producers by their hot little hands and cooperate." Her advice, for once unhappily, went unheeded. And when E. F. MacDonald, president of Zenith, announced at a 1950 press conference that the deluxe motion picture theater was doomed through stagnation at the box office and that Hollywood should at once start to manufacture films for the box, his remarks were dismissed by many industry chiefs. The whole, current concept of Phonevision, in which an additional $1 on the phone bill ensured the showing of a current-release movie, was quashed by industry indifference.

Television for theaters (known as Eidophor), Phonevision, Hollywood vs. New York TV production: the controversial issues dragged on for years, while the audience gradually drained away, and year by year the moguls' pronouncements of 1950 seemed more hollow and foolishly fearless. Nicholas Schenck of MGM was quoted as saying in a roundup of industry opinions by Ezra Goodman (New York *Daily News*, January 25, 1950): "So far television hasn't hurt the box office. Good pictures do business as always." Gradwell Sears of United Artists dismissed the medium with the remark that "TV is just another way of selling soap, cigarettes or Mad Man Muntz." Only Barney Balaban of Paramount, with characteristic foresight, saw that "TV could be a superb medium for advertising and publicizing the Hollywood product." Had he foreseen what it took Hollywood almost twenty years to find out—that movies for TV were obviously the answer to the industry's ills—he would have done even better. Instead, he and the other industry chiefs began to seek, in 1950–53, other ways in which to combat the terrifying new giant. Their answer lay in wide screens.

7

In 1952, when the wide-screen revolution began, Nicholas Schenck continued to lord it over MGM. Harry, Albert and Jack Warner were still in command of their studio, Barney Balaban, Spyros Skouras, and Harry Cohn were firmly enthroned at Paramount, Fox, and Columbia. Late in 1951, even those most contemptuous of television realized that the public's desertion of motion pictures was growing to an alarming degree and began to look for a formula that might save their threatened heads. The shareholders were after their blood; their own political pusillanimity had deprived them of some of their major talents; one by one the theater chains were being wrested from them. Was there a way out of the blind alley, or was Hollywood doomed?

First of all, means had to be found of surviving the Department of Justice's rulings. Behind the scenes, a reshuffle occurred so that, as a typical example, one studio would book its entire product into a rival's severed chain. Another way around the problem, clearly, would be to develop wide screen, which would be indispensable to the theater chains—forcing them to install it through whole areas of the country once public acceptance had been achieved. Thus, a greedy small chain which had forced the severance of a greedy large one would be forced into a position of having to please its customers by installing a new screen system, and at one stroke something approaching the situation before the abolition of block-booking and consent decrees could be achieved.

This motivation, not always fully conscious but running like an invisible stream through the more obvious labyrinthine negotiations of those early anti-TV struggles, called for a system that would excite, dazzle, and drag the millions back from the comfort of their homes. It was with an acute awareness of this that in 1952 various enterprises began to develop 3-D film in the hope of saving and revolutionizing the industry.

Three-dimensional film had had a surprisingly long history. Aside from tentative experiments by William Friese-Greene in 1893, and by Edison during the first decade of the century, the most effective work in the field was done by the president of Chicago's Essanay Studios, George K. Spoor. A mild-eyed, plumpish, rather undistinguished-looking man, Spoor pursued his dream of 3-D with an extraordinary resolution. Spoor's NaturalVision, worked out with the aid of a Swedish scientist, Paul Berggren, showed the image on two adjoining screens, one of which appeared to illustrate the foreground and the other the background of a given image. After years of experiments, most of them disastrous, the first public demonstration was given in Los Angeles in September, 1926. Shortly after that, the stereoscopic process was applied to a mediocre feature film, *Danger Lights,* co-starring Jean Arthur and Louis Wolheim. The public found the split-screen effect unsettling—in the cities it was a tolerable oddity, but in the Midwest and deep South it was not enjoyed at all. Later, George Spoor tried another venture in short films, but by the mid-1930s it was clear that his efforts were commercially doomed.

During the same period, at least a dozen further inventions had been patented. Of these, the most satisfactory was the anaglyph process, in which two cameras shot a scene and the spectator seemed to be looking at one image by means of spectacles with red and green lenses. Edwin S. Porter, who directed *The Great Train Robbery*, created a special anaglyph program as early as 1915, featuring country scenes and shots of Niagara Falls. In 1922, a film called *The Power of Love*, with Elliott Sparling and Barbara Bedford, appeared. It was presented by a pioneer named Harry K. Flirall and did not achieve a wide release, despite an enthusiastic initial reception at the Ambassador Theatre in Los Angeles. Several experiments later, anaglyph reappeared at its most spectacular in the celebrated Pete Smith Audioscopiks of the 1930s. Trains screamed across the audience, waters rushed overhead, and arrows flew from Indian bows. Aesthetically the equal of a roller-coaster ride, the experience won few critical adherents and the necessity to use special glasses fazed the audience. Two years after the second—and last—Audioscopiks in 1938, MGM prepared a spoof horror film, *Three Dimension Murder*, directed by George Sidney. It was not a success.

Anaglyph was complemented by the Polaroid system, also inviting the use of special glasses, and virtually identical in its results. Edwin Land and George Wheelwright, Jr., together developed Polaroid lenses, and at the New York World's Fair in 1939 presented a film in which a Chrysler automobile assembled itself to a musical accompaniment. After a long lapse, Polaroid 3-D re-emerged at the Festival of Britain in 1951, with ballets and Norman McLaren animated shorts taking pride of place. It was later the same year that a little-known journalist, Milton Gunzburg, aided by his ophthalmologist brother, Julian, really established Polaroid 3-D as a viable proposition.

Quietly energetic and heavy-set, with slightly slanting, edgy, blue-gray eyes, Gunzburg had had a moderately successful career as a journalist—editing a *New York Times* magazine supplement, working on the *Los Angeles Times*—and a screenwriter (*Sister Kenny, Tennessee Johnson*) before he became seized by an idea that rapidly became an obsession. His wife, heiress to a dairy fortune, luckily stood by him as he plunged more and more of his savings into experiments, based largely on the pioneer work of a cameraman named Friend Baker, who had sold him his patent application for a nominal sum and a small percentage of any accruing profits.

Baker's 3-D Natural Vision camera was composed of two 35mm Mitchells, mounted with lenses facing each other, each lens focusing on an adjustable mirror at an angle of 45 degrees. The mirrors were worked by hand controls to swing like human eyes and converge their fields of vision to the same point. The cameras were focused individually but shot scenes in unison. Two projectors were needed to show them on the screen, each filtering through a Polaroid screen. Polaroid glasses provided a unified image.

Gunzburg bought Friend Baker's patent application and had the first camera built in a machine shop. At first, the costs were estimated at $50,000, but these escalated to $230,000. After a series of trial-and-error experiments, he had ten of them made, and these were satisfactory. The gamble was all or nothing. Gunzburg's father put up $5,000, his mother-in-law $10,000, Julian Gunzburg $5,000, and Milton Gunzburg his life's savings of $10,000. Gunzburg began by photographing hot-rod cars with the new cameras, running off the experimental footage in a private theater. He took over a studio on the corner of La Brea and Hollywood Boulevard and began making sequences with actors, testing projectors to make sure that they were flawless. His plan for making a hot-rod 3-D movie vanished when he realized that the funds intended for it were already being fully absorbed.

Then came a really serious blow. Only Polaroid had sufficient resources to make the glasses with which an audience could view 3-D. When Gunzburg approached the Polaroid Company, placing an order for thousands of viewers, he was turned down flat. He telephoned them frantically. A company representative said that a deal had already been made with the producer Lester Cowan, who intended making a musical, the last sequence of which would be shot in 3-D, with Al Jolson singing to introduce the new medium as he had introduced the talkies.

After all his months of work and the full commitment of his family's financial resources, Gunzburg thought the end had come. Luckily for him, a family friend, Sterling Pile, was on the board of Polaroid, handling its affairs directly with Wall Street. Gunzburg told him what had happened and pleaded for help. Polaroid stretched a point, and let him into the club. The contract excluded the unfortunate Lester Cowan and indicated that, provided Gunzburg bought their entire supply of viewers, he could have exclusive rights to use them for six months followed by an option to renew, which Polaroid would exercise.

Gunzburg still needed $50,000 to proceed and make his picture, but the money proved impossible to obtain. He signed away his home and all of his possessions, including his wife's family estate, an enormous mansion on Sunset Boulevard. All that was left—since further private funds could not be obtained—was to go to the studios and hope to attract some interest there.

At 20th Century-Fox, an executive, Lou Anger, who handled personal enterprises for the studio's production chief, Joe Schenck, and for its chairman, Spyros Skouras, showed an interest, and so did Charles Skouras, who ran the Fox Theatre chains and had formerly had Gunzburg's father-in-law on the board. At a party, Charles Skouras flung his arms around Gunzburg in a bear hug and expressed enormous enthusiasm for 3-D. Spyros Skouras saw some scenes and immediately gave Gunzburg a six-month verbal—but nonfinancial—option, one which, in Gunzburg's words, "only a jerk would accept." The Skourases named many important pictures which they wanted to adapt to 3-D, and he believed them, but none of the plans materialized. At the end of six months Gunzburg was nearing bankruptcy and still not one inch off the ground.

Finally, Gunzburg's nerves snapped. He told the Skourases he could wait no longer, and instead went to MGM, where he had worked in the forties as a writer. With the aid of an attorney who knew Eddie Mannix, head of production in Hollywood, he showed some footage. Mannix was enthusiastic, and so was Louis B. Mayer. They almost immediately decided to shoot *Kiss Me Kate,* a version of Cole Porter's musical with Howard Keel and Kathryn Grayson, in Gunzburg's 3-D system. But before the absolutely final decision could be made, Gunzburg must show the footage to the company's chief, Nicholas Schenck, in New York.

Schenck immediately arranged a private screening, run by the man in charge of projection for Loew's Theatres. Among those present was George Schaefer, former head of RKO, who had brought Orson Welles to Hollywood. Schaefer had a verbal agreement with Gunzburg to act as distributors' representative when 3-D finally came into the theaters. As Schenck, Schaefer, Gunzburg, and the others present sank into their seats, an appalling thing happened. The film ran backwards, showing cars reversing off the screen into space. Nicholas Schenck didn't wait for Gunzburg's frantic explanations. Patting him condescendingly on the shoulder, he said, "Young man, I think you have something. But you're not quite ready yet!"

Gradually, in those hard months of 1951 Gunzburg realized

that all the moguls were trying to do was to wear him down, hoping that in time he would drop the whole concept of 3-D. They believed that 3-D would render the flat film obsolete and ruin their prospects with even the planned wider screens of the future. He took out a bank loan, using as collateral the remnants of his property, and started to make plans to make the hot-rod feature after all. He renewed his contract with Polaroid to the tune of $50,000. At that moment Arch Oboler, an independent film-maker who had made a name as a radio writer, approached him with the idea of making an African adventure picture, *Bwana Devil*, as a 3-D venture.

Enormously energetic and dynamic, Oboler convinced Gunzburg that he should let him make the film. The production was among the worst of all movies, patched together from new 35mm and old blown-up 16mm footage shot in Africa, and poorly played by Robert Stack and Barbara Britton. With only $10,000 as a starting fund, Oboler called people in every day to see the rushes and invest enough money to make the next day's shooting possible. Piece by piece, the production was built up, until at last something approaching a releasable feature emerged.

The Polaroid executives were horrified when they saw the picture, as was Gunzburg; he felt that it would severely damage his name. Worse than the problems of the picture itself were the poor projections of its sample footage at industry screenings. Even though Gunzburg had only 20 percent of the picture, he felt an obligation to make sure that every screening was perfect and became involved in endless wrangles to that end. George J. Schaefer, with his many industry contacts, managed to smooth various executives' ruffled brows and finally sold the picture to United Artists, which opened the picture through the former Paramount chain.

The premiere in Hollywood was followed by a massive party at Gunzburg's wife's family mansion, now mortgaged to the hilt. The best reactions showed only an embarrassed politeness, and Marco Wolfe, head of the Paramount chain, told Gunzburg, "There's one way you'll know if you've made it. Tomorrow, the box office will open at 11 A.M. If there's nobody at the box office you'll know it hasn't hit. If there are two you'll know you've got a chance. If you've got ten there, you may really have something."

Next morning, Gunzburg and his wife stayed in bed, unwilling to face daylight. She said to him, "We can be ruined. Did you ever think of that?" At 11 A.M. Gunzburg decided to call the theater. The morning-paper reviews had been terrible, and he feared the worst. It was the most momentous telephone call of his life.

When he got through, the manager paused for a moment, while Gunzburg's soul dribbled slowly through his bedroom slippers. Then the manager said, "My God! They're lined up down the block all the way to the Gotham Delicatessen! It's the most incredible thing I've ever seen! And downtown they're lined up all around the block as well!"

On Monday—the picture had opened on Friday—Jack Warner called Gunzburg and offered him a two-picture deal. It was typical of Warner's prescience that he should have foreseen the enormous potential of the medium just as he had foreseen the possibilities of talkies twenty-six years earlier. As soon as they received word of Warner's interest, Arch Oboler and George Schaefer insisted they buy out of their contract and arrange a separate contract which would permit them to make saturation bookings of the picture (Gunzburg having insisted on restricting distribution to twenty-five theaters to ensure high projection standards). Almost at once, *Bwana Devil,* as the studio's first 3-D venture, became a great success, netting an immense fortune for all concerned with it.

At Warners, an extraordinary situation developed. Settling on a remake of *The Mystery of the Wax Museum,* with the new title *House of Wax,* Jack Warner chose as its director one of the handful of Hollywood craftsmen unable to see 3-D: Andre de Toth, one-eyed husband of Veronica Lake. After three days of work, Gunzburg panicked and began supervising the director with Jack Warner's permission; De Toth, he felt, not only had no idea how to see in three dimensions, he didn't know how to shoot to convey depth of field.

His fears were groundless. *House of Wax,* brilliantly photographed by J. Peverell Marley, became an overwhelming success, and a mass panic set in. There was a good deal of talk in executive circles that Gunzburg wanted to take over the industry, using his patent rights and his Polaroid contract to hold everyone very firmly over a barrel. Warners rushed ahead into its 3-D Western, *The Charge at Feather River,* with arrows, firebrands, and even actor Frank Lovejoy's spittle hurtling into the audience. Studio after studio began turning over its worst screenplays and its worst directors to the new medium instead of using their best materials, and before long 3-D was a glut on the market. Projections, too, became less and less adequate, due to hurried and inefficient methods, and complaints of eyestrain were legion: Gunzburg himself even manned the projector for *Bwana Devil's* New York opening.

"Three Dimentia" seized Hollywood. Dore Schary told *Time* (March 2, 1953): "Third dimension provides the industry with a wonderful opportunity to tell stories in new ways!" Sidney Skolsky was painfully accurate in his note of caution: "The movie industry, like a man running to a quack doctor, tries to find a quick cure-all . . . a hypo of 3-D. . . . Well, the industry will have to face and fight its original fear and frustration." The producer Jerry Wald sounded cheerful: "I'm enthusiastic about anything that calls attention to Hollywood—3-D, three colors, three legs or two —if they're Marilyn Monroe's," while the comedian George

(87)

Jessel dismissed the whole fad with the words: "I predict that one year from now the studios will be making nothing but glasses."

In their rush to get into 3-D, the moguls tried to wrest the exclusive Polaroid-glasses contract away from Gunzburg and have it placed in the exclusive provenance of National Screen Service, a distributing organization which handled trailers for the entire industry. Pressure was put upon Polaroid, which had several board members also engaged in various executive capacities in the industry. Already distressed by *Bwana Devil* and by the poor projection generally available, Charles Skouras arranged for the Research Council to change the screen standards, rendering Gunzburg's equipment worthless.

Charles Skouras called Gunzburg over to him at the big industry first screening of CinemaScope, hugged him, and told him with his most amiable smile that he was going to wreck his business, making CinemaScope the standard. "He was the smiler with the knife. He killed me with the hug," Gunzburg says.

MGM panicked again, deciding not to launch its *Kiss Me Kate* firmly in 3-D but rather try it in both flat and in-depth versions in different cities to see where the strongest reaction would be. *Kiss Me Kate* opened at Radio City Music Hall in 3-D and flopped. The death blow came for Milton Gunzburg and he decided to get out; Polaroid settled his contract for an immense sum.

He wasn't able to enter a peaceful life at once, however. In October, 1953, George J. Schaefer brought a $3,500,000 suit against him, his wife, Vera, Julian and Samuel Gunzburg, Mrs. Rose Burch, and Natural Vision Theatre Equipment Corporation, charging that Gunzburg had entered into a contract which gave him equal shares in the 3-D process, but that he had formed three corporations and issued stock to his relatives, thereby depriving Schaefer of his share of the profits. This, he claimed, violated the terms of his contract. He asked for a share of the profits, an accounting of profits, appointment of a receiver to take over the business, and a dissolution of the corporation. Federal Judge Ben Harrison rejected the partnership portion of the suit in October, 1955, after three weeks of trial. Gunzburg, it was alleged, made $3,750,000 from the sale of glasses, and the Gunzburg firm's profits were estimated at between $60 and $80 million.

Arthur Groman, attorney for Milton Gunzburg, charged breach of fiduciary trust on Schaefer's part, alleging that Schaefer, then representing Guly Productions (*Bwana Devil*), and Edward Alperson for Warners and UA, had failed to act properly in the negotiations. Schaefer admitted he had never filed the necessary partnership reports, and the case was thrown out of court. But it cost Gunzburg $150,000 to win it.

Understandably, Milton Gunzburg had had enough of the film industry by then. Retiring with his fortune, he settled in Puerto Vallarta, Mexico, where he lives today. Contented though he is, he regrets the fact that 3-D's career lasted barely twelve months. Exploited, used as a trick, and rapidly shelved, 3-D only in 1972 had begun to be revived.

8

Long before Milton Gunzburg's professional destruction and the termination of 3-D, and long before CinemaScope became accepted as the standard, another rival system had arisen which could not so easily be challenged. This was Cinerama, for all its drawbacks still the most excitingly spectacular medium for large-screen epics, too often thrown away on merely gimmicky fairground excitements.

The creator of Cinerama—he barely survived its inception, and died only two years after its first screenings—was Fred Waller, a shy, gangling, absentminded genius whose entire career was devoted to an obscure struggle to develop various new film devices. Little known in his time and now totally forgotten, he was a classic example of the inventor whose lack of personal glamor and magnetism and inability to exploit his own talent led to years of near poverty and a dark struggle to pursue his vision. All his life, financiers were captivated by his experiments, but withdrew just when those experiments seemed about to come to fruition. He was the victim of impatience, of overenthusiasm without a sense of responsibility, and of the unloving world of the movie business itself, to which he was utterly unsuited.

Gunzburg's enthusiasm, burning though it undoubtedly was, flared and faded within a couple of years, but Waller's was a lifetime preoccupation. From the first he had been aggravated by the confines of the small screen. Born in Brooklyn in 1887, he was driven by an obsession to leave school before graduation and work at a dozen jobs to save the money to make still photographs. At nineteen he was involved in preparing displays of stills for nickelodeon lobbies, and at the age of twenty-six he had become a supplier of pre-prepared still displays for theaters across the country. Later he became a cinematographer, helped form the Film Guild, and worked with the director Frank Tuttle. In 1921 he joined Paramount Studios, working under its chief, Jesse L. Lasky, in the preparation of special photographic effects. His absentminded charm made him immensely popular there, precursor of the brilliant Farciot Edouart of later years. He staged rain storms, shipwrecks, and fires with great panache, achieving his most delightfully bizarre effects in the storm that set the castaways adrift in Cecil B. DeMille's *Male and Female*. He spent his spare time working at special lenses that could roughly approximate the range of the human eye and bring spectacular scenes to the audience with unusual, glittering vividness.

Among Waller's 167 patents were those for water skis and a device whereby a tailor could photograph the entire human figure stereoscopically for suit-measuring purposes. Before talkies he left Paramount to concentrate with relentless single-mindedness on wide-screen alone. He settled in a comfortable, rambling house with a tennis court near Oyster Bay, New York, sinking his carefully preserved funds into a series of enormous new screens.

In 1937, Waller's experiments attracted the attention

of the architectural firm Voorhees, Walker, Foley, and Smith, which asked him to prepare a curved-screen film for projection inside a sphere at the 1939 New York World's Fair.

The system Waller developed—Vitorama—was made up of eleven cameras and eleven projectors and produced a bizarre, multi-imaged result rather like seeing the world through the eyes of a fly. Later, the millionaire financier Laurance Rockefeller bought a half share in the invention and presented Waller with some old stables owned by the family as a place for experiments. In World War II, Waller worked for the government, devising a brilliantly effective aerial gunnery training system, in which five projectors threw images of enemy planes on a screen. A trainee could fire at his attackers while seated on a revolving chair inside a giant glass dome like the identical part of a warplane. As he hit an attacking aircraft, the trainee's earphones obediently bleeped. The results were so effective that countless lives were saved.

In 1946, Waller developed special film displays for *Life* magazine's "New America" exhibition. Laurance Rockefeller, Hazard Reeves—a superb sound engineer who worked on the invention—and *Time* magazine together helped form Cinerama Corp. For three years Waller worked desperately hard to perfect the system. He finally developed a more sophisticated three-lensed camera and three projectors, but the system still seemed cumbersome, and *Time* and Rockefeller withdrew, leaving the company almost in ruins. The company was liquidated, and Waller was convinced his career was over.

But he reckoned without the extraordinary determination of Hazard Reeves, the sound engineer, who formed Cinerama, Inc., pouring $60,000 of his own into the new company and selling new batches of shares at $2.00 each. Reeves then traveled the country seeking the cooperation of film backers and film companies. For months a parade of celebrated financiers and studio chiefs arrived at Waller's Oyster Bay home and watched the gigantic crude images unfold over his outdoor tennis court. Delighted, frequently applauding as excitedly as children, no one was willing to invest a cent in it. Then, in 1950, one visitor listened.

His name was Lowell Thomas. The famous broadcaster, traveler, and author was deeply impressed, and with his business manager, Frank Smith, succeeded in raising money from Roberts and Company, the investment company, Paul V. Kesten of CBS, and the financier Alger B. Chapan. Louis B. Mayer, recently ousted from MGM after years of struggle with Nicholas Schenck, became head of the company and a major stockholder.

Despite Thomas's enthusiastic promotional speeches and appeals to the big companies, most of the majors turned Cincrama down flat. Nicholas Schenck, aggravated by Mayer's comeback, rejected the system out of hand. Spyros Skouras and Darryl F. Zanuck felt it was too expensive to mass market. A series of executives made the journey to Oyster Bay, enjoyed an excellent dinner prepared by Waller's wife, settled down under the stars and enjoyed the triptych of three vast images spread against the sky. They shook Waller's hand —and he heard no more from them.

Finally, Lowell Thomas's passionate interest in Cinerama sparked off that of one film-maker, his friend the producer Merian C. Cooper, who with Ernest Schoedsack had made the immortal *King Kong*. Cooper and Thomas together had frequent viewings on Waller's tennis court, and finally they decided to launch the process together. Cooper worked thirty-six hour shifts to cut the film, adapting his veteran's editing technique to the demands of the new medium.

The first New York presentation of *This Is Cinerama,* at the Broadway Theatre on September 30, 1952, was an enormous success. The audience screamed with masochistic pleasure as it was plunged down a Coney Island roller coaster or sent flying through the Grand Canyon. The fact that the sides of the screen jiggled, giving a disagreeable sense of vertigo to more sensitive viewers, seemed to disconcert no critic, and at times the three images actually jelled: particularly when the three glass panels of a bomber's nose exactly matched the triptych on the screen. Hazard Reeves' sound had a deafening magnificence: the screech of plane wheels, the slurp of water of a Venetian gondola, the roar of the roller-coaster crowd. Reviews were uniformly enthusiastic. But Louis B. Mayer expressed a note of caution when he told a Hollywood Screen Producers' Guild Award dinner that Cinerama might have a limited future, that no more than two hundred theaters would be able to equip with it in the following three years. He was right, though his remarks scarcely made him popular with the board of directors.

Evidently sensing severe competition, Milton Gunzburg in late September charged Cinerama with improperly using the term 3-D in their advertisements. In an attorney's letter he cautioned the New York company to avoid such misrepresentation in future. It was a vain ploy: 3-D was already even at this early stage outmatched by its massive rival. Cinerama did not require special glasses. As the magazine *Fortnight* remarked, "That gorgeous blonde brushes the Cinerama moviegoer with a love-size kiss. The ladies can almost feel the arms of Tarzan, the breath of Don Juan." Plans, few of them fulfilled, were announced for feature-length Cinerama pictures—a musical, a Western, and a fantasy in the manner of *King Kong. Paint Your Wagon*—not made for sixteen years—was announced for 1953, to be followed by *Joseph and His Brethren* and *Blossom Time*.

Cinerama proceeded boldly, undeterred by such rude remarks as *Look* magazine's that the system reminded it of a Mississippi painting made by a man in the 1840s. The painting was three miles wide.

Early in 1953, Jack Warner began serious discussions with Cinerama on producing two features a year.

By April 26, Cinerama had grossed more than $100,000 and by December $10,000,000. It was obvious that satisfactory new rivals to 3-D, Cinerama, and television were needed. The first of these was CinemaScope.

While 3-D presented its eyestrain problems and Cinerama was evidently going to be too costly to install in every city and town in the country, CinemaScope quite clearly was a more than effective answer to both. As early as 1913 a frail, struggling academic, Henry Chrétien, developed the special lens which squeezed down and widened the image to the proportions of a letter-box slit. In the early talkie period, during a wide-screen vogue, he tried without success to market his invention in the United States. Paramount—the only company interested—failed to maintain its option. By 1953, forty years after he had created the lens, he was still, with incredible tenacity, demonstrating it in Paris at the Optical Institute and the Sorbonne, where he taught his devoted students.

In the fall of 1952, Spyros Skouras, chairman of 20th Century-Fox, was in Australia and the Far East on a series of discussions with his offices in Sydney and Tokyo. A broad, slow-speaking, solidly aggressive polar bear of a man, he had risen from poverty-stricken Greek origins to immense wealth developing shipping interests and theater chains. In 1942, after assuming control of the Fox Theatres, Skouras took over the presidency of the studios from the late Sidney Kent, and by 1951 he had carried it successfully through a series of crises, maintaining technical standards higher than those of any other studio in Hollywood.

It was obvious, though, by 1952, that Fox under Skouras, dynamic, unsleeping and limitlessly ambitious though he was, had begun to run out of steam, and television was growing. Seeing its potential, he tried to buy the ABC network, but his board declared itself unconvinced, believed television would crash, and forebade the deal. New gimmicks were needed to keep the studio vigorous. First Skouras tried to market the Eidophor system of closed-circuit TV shown on theater screens, but this had only a limited success. His lavish publicity campaign under the banner "Movies Are Better Than Ever" provided only a temporary fillip. He was never more than half-hearted about 3-D in the days before he helped swat it for good. Something else was needed, and he began looking desperately for it.

Returning from that Far Eastern trip late in 1952, Skouras stopped off in Switzerland to talk with Earl Sponable, head of the 20th Century-Fox research department, about the closed-circuit TV developments. The conversation was slow, and Skouras, already bored with a day's discussions with the Swiss Eidophor people on the closed-circuit idea and realizing it wasn't working too well, nodded off to sleep. Sponable went on talking, and suddenly something he said made Skouras sit up with a start: "That Frenchman's lens is really something!"

The normally laconic Sponable explained enthusiastically that the lens, now thoroughly sophisticated, compressed a photographed image, squeezing it out on a wide ratio, while a special projection lens would transfer it to the screen. Skouras was overjoyed with the idea and tossed and turned all night.

"Next morning," Skouras told me in 1971 at his Mamaroneck, New York, home, "I came sleepily to breakfast. Then Sponable dropped a bombshell. He said, casually, 'Oh, by the way, J. Arthur Rank in England has an option on the invention.' I said, 'After a sleepless night, now you tell me.' But then Sponable added, 'It only has days to run.'

"We flew to Paris in an agony of suspense. Thank God, the option expired and Rank didn't renew. That was on a Wednesday. On Thursday I told the Fox Newsreel team in Paris to use the Chrétien lenses for a demonstration. Then on Saturday a small group of us sat down at the back of the balcony in the big Rex Theatre and waited.

"The curtain parted and my heart turned over. I knew this was the greatest thing I had ever seen. When the monuments of Paris, the Arc de Triomphe, the Eiffel Tower, the trees of the Bois de Boulogne appeared wide-screen, I went crazy and grabbed every telephone in sight.

"I flew at once to New York and the guys there loved the system. Al Lichtman, who handled our exhibition, loved it more than anyone—he'd always been bitterly disappointed that the engineers told us not to get into Cinerama. I went to Hollywood."

Skouras arrived home in Hollywood, flung his arms around Zanuck, and told him he had seen the most wonderful invention of a lifetime. Zanuck immediately told Sol Halprin, head of the 20th Century-Fox camera department, and the three men, after a series of conferences, decided to shoot the fully prepared spectacle *The Robe* in the new system, as well as in normal ratio. Halprin immediately turned over every spare man to preparing a demonstration reel in the new system while—due to the pressing schedule—the normal ratio *The Robe* began shooting. They had at the time only one of Chrétien's lenses; the others were being cut in Paris. Halprin shot a scenic railway sequence at Long Beach, mounting the camera in one of the cars in a whirling device known as a Cyclone. The camera began to bounce badly as the Cyclone began to revolve, and Halprin and the crew were terrified the precious lens would be damaged; they hung on grimly at each twist of the rails. After several hazardous journeys they finally achieved a number of superb participation shots. An intention to mount the camera in an auto speed race at Culver City fizzled out when it was discovered the cameras would be severely damaged in the process.

Halprin flew in a bomber over Yosemite National Park, achieving some impressive close shots of snow-covered peaks. Skouras and Zanuck were delighted with these, and decided to take the most extraordinary gamble in screen history: they

(97)

would mortgage the entire studio, the backlot, and the real estate which they then owned by turning over the entire production lineup to CinemaScope and borrowing scores of millions from the banks—led by the Chase Manhattan and the Bank of America. The contract for further improved lenses with the Bausch and Lomb Company alone amounted to $30 million.

For Halprin, the major problem the system presented was that it had a soft fuzziness at the sides of the frame, a fuzziness which could be offset by lighting carefully. Leon Shamroy, a master of color, was engaged to handle the first features, and although he detested CinemaScope because it widened and distorted faces in closeup and diffused the fine sharpness of the color process, he struggled manfully with its countless problems.

The decision to make *The Robe* the first CinemaScope film was largely brought about by the personal enterprise of the producer, Frank Ross. A handsome, determined, immensely energetic man, Ross had been obsessed with the idea of filming Lloyd C. Douglas's sanctimonious, Bible-belt best seller for more than a decade. He had first learned of the novel in 1942. While mowing the lawn of his neighbor, the Broadway producer Richard Halliday, he got wind of it from an overheard conversation of Halliday's. He immediately plunged most of his financial resources—$100,000—into buying the property for the screen, working for years with the German novelist Gina Kaus, with the scenarist Philip Dunne, and several others on the script. Originally, the production was to have been made at RKO, but successive RKO production chiefs shelved the project, until finally in 1952 Darryl F. Zanuck and Spyros Skouras bought RKO's interest.

Gregory Peck, Laurence Olivier, Tyrone Power, Gary Cooper, and Robert Taylor were all mentioned as possibilities for the leading role of the soldier who won Christ's robe in a dice game. DeMille, Victor Fleming, and Mervyn LeRoy were named as directors—DeMille in particular being anxious to handle it (the subject was ready-made for him). Finally, Ross, Zanuck, and Skouras settled on a comparatively obscure player, Richard Burton, to act the leading role: his sturdy figure, clear-cut features and blue eyes had already made their mark on the English stage, and after a series of interviews Ross decided he had sufficient appeal to carry the picture.

Lyle Wheeler, Fox's set designer, created a handsome $275,000 slave market, a hill of Golgotha, a splendid Roman bath, the catacombs where the Christians fled to escape their persecutors, the marble palace of Caligula, a Roman torture chamber, slave galleys, and the gates of Jerusalem.

Like Gunzburg's venture into 3-D, this was an all-or-nothing gamble. Skouras announced that every one of the studio's sixteen sound stages must be used, and that in future every single Fox picture would be made in CinemaScope: if the public did not like it, then the studio would be destroyed almost overnight.

Shooting sensibly was confined to local settings, converted to the perfect authenticity of which Fox had always been proud, but one piece of realism nearly cost two of the leading players their lives. A fire broke out, caused by the upsetting of a painstakingly accurate first-century brazier filled with real olive oil. The flaring oil fell onto a highly inflammable, authentic silk canopy over the heads of Richard Burton and Victor Mature and they only just escaped with minor burns. Jeff Morrow was injured in a duel scene, and Jean Simmons, as a simple Christian girl in love with Richard Burton's Marcellus, knocked herself out cold when she ran at him in a love scene and her chin collided with his all too solidly accurate Roman breastplate.

Rushed through in a mere handful of weeks that spring of 1953, the picture caused an overwhelming public response. Lines ran around the blocks in the cities, and the mixture of religiosity, sex, husky men and frail women, and unadulterated corn worked effortlessly, dragging the majority of God-fearing Americans in by the scruff of their necks. The critics, equally predictably, carped: *The New Yorker*'s John McCarten, most hated of the New York reviewers within the industry before the advent of Pauline Kael and John Simon, said, "The actors in close-ups look as if they belonged on Mount Rushmore." Britain added critiques: *The Manchester Guardian* rudely said that "the fate of the film industry [through CinemaScope] depends now on parental pride rather than on prophetic vision." *The Times* found it "a prolonged battery of the eye and ear, disturbing the judgment. It is not 3-D, although it gives some illusion of depth. It is, as it were, 2½ D." *The Sunday Express* said that "watching both ends, or trying to, gives you a touch of Wimbledon neck." *The Daily Mail* said that CinemaScope merely made "distastefulness wider" and *The Observer* that "the effect on the viewer is to make him feel he is sitting inside a monster mail box looking out through the slot at a world roughly in the proportions of a Dachshund."

Throughout the world, from Europe to Australia and New Zealand, the reaction was roughly the same, but nobody in Hollywood really cared. And it was obviously only a question of time before every studio had turned over the bulk of its product to CinemaScope. Walt Disney announced three features and several shorts in the new process, including *Lady and the Tramp,* and Jules Verne's *20,000 Leagues Under the Sea.* In June, Skouras (who had been in and out of Europe seemingly every other week, doing without sleep and carried by a ferocious native energy) rushed back from London to Hollywood to tell his executives that the Siemans–Halske electronic equipment firm in Germany would immediately produce 250 stereophonic sound sets a month and that the European exhibitors were hugely enthusiastic following an initial demonstration in Paris.

Then Skouras ran into a major snag. He told me: "After the successful demonstration film in Hollywood—5,000 people were there—I immediately ordered 250 cameras and 3,000 lenses from Chrétien, but he went down with double pneumonia and I had to rule that out as hopeless. So in desperation I flew to Rochester, New York, and spoke to the Bausch and Lomb lens people, asking for an immediate answer: Could they supply us with that number of lenses to Chrétien's specifications by July? They asked me to call back a few hours later, while I sweated it out. At last they said 'Yes.' When I got back to New York the board asked how much the lenses would cost. When I said $150,000 to $5 million they nearly died, but they finally agreed. Finally the bill for the first seventy-five lenses came in. Our treasurer, Henderson, looked white. I said, 'Pay it.' It was for $575,000!"

The Hollywood Reporter echoed the bullish optimism of the period, as strong as that of 1946, in a front-page editorial:

> We've seen the new Cinemascope!
> We've heard the new Eastern Stereophonic Sound!
> We've viewed the new Crystal Clear Eastman color stock!
> The combination of the three . . . is the answer to every exhibitor's prayer. This is it boys. You can toss away the Polaroids!

By December 31, *The Robe* had already netted $16 million in four hundred theaters, and 1,500 CinemaScope installations in the United States and Canada had taken place— only eleven months after the first three Chrétien lenses had been flown from Paris to New York on January 18. That December also, three new CinemaScope pictures were in release: *How to Marry a Millionaire,* Jean Negulesco's version of the countlessly remade story of three girls out to trap wealthy men, *Beneath the Twelve-Mile Reef,* a story of divers in the Caribbean, and *King of the Khyber Rifles,* a spectacle ostensibly set in India. Warner Brothers, after futilely trying to mass-market WarnerScope and Warner-SuperScope, gave in that fall and agreed to join the rush into CinemaScope. Finally, only Paramount, which had been offered, obtained an option on, but had failed to use Chrétien's lens in 1933 and again in 1946, stuck out firmly against the new system.

In 1954 the industry was flushed with excitement following an astonishing new prosperity. Other systems were under way: Mike Todd's Todd-AO, the most famous of these, though Paramount's neglected VistaVision (the film going horizontally through the projector), with unusually fine-grained images achieved in such films as Anthony Mann's *Strategic Air Command*, offered the more brilliant and beautiful effects.

Strategic Air Command, with its shots through a bomber's plexiglass nose, its drifting, crimson clouds at sunset and glistening blue skies sliced by silver metal wings, was a revelation of VistaVision's potential. It far surpassed CinemaScope's more popular but shallower and fuzzier look. "Those Bausch and Lomb lenses were hell" was a typical remark of Leon Shamroy, photographer of *The Robe*. But, he added, "CinemaScope may have ruined the art of motion pictures for a decade; it also saved the industry." At least for a time, wide-screen made Hollywood still possible, and for the next five years the gimmicks (including Smellovision) were endless.

Zanuck made contracts with MGM (a reluctant Nicholas Schenck finally saw the light), Columbia, Universal, and all the other studios except Paramount. The reason Paramount failed to adopt CinemaScope, with damaging results in loss of revenue, seems to have been a very odd one. Due to an oversight, Y. Frank Freeman, head of the studio at the time, had not been invited to the first of the private demonstrations of CinemaScope for industry chiefs. He apparently believed that the slight was intended to refer directly to the fact that Paramount simply wanted to fight what looked like a complete Fox takeover of the entire film industry, and an escape from the Department of Justice's rulings, since CinemaScope would now be the norm.

One theater chain was willing to make its complaint heard in a public statement at the end of 1953. The Allied States Association of Motion Picture Exhibitors issued a bulletin charging that the promotion of CinemaScope presented "the boldest attempt to dominate the industry by means of a gadget since William Fox threatened it with the Tri-Ergon sound patents." The Association believed that not all exhibitors would be able to adapt to CinemaScope ratio and they would be forced out of business if they could not. In fact, many theaters did close down in the months that followed.

In many ways, the use of the new technique rendered academic the Department of Justice's inconvenient severance rulings, since the Fox theaters, run by Spyros Skouras' brother Charles, by paying for Fox equipment, were in fact simply plowing back money into the former associated company, a situation as satisfactory as that of block-bookings. The rest of the industry for three years was dominated by Fox. Although CinemaScope ostensibly was just an answer to television, it was the answer to Washington as well. Once more a guaranteed series of outlets existed for products, because no one could fail to show CinemaScope if they wanted to stay in business after the public's overwhelming acceptance of *The Robe* and its successors, *How to Marry a Millionaire* and *Beneath the Twelve-Mile Reef*. It had only been a brief time since the Department of Justice had made its final rulings and since the overwhelming success of television, but now the big top was going up again—the future suddenly looked sharply bright.

9

As CinemaScope began to dominate the whole industry and more and more exhibitors fought a fight to install the new image and sound equipment, a whole rash of systems emerged. In the wake of VistaVision and its accompanying Paramount process Paravision, the studios presented Vanascope, Vista-rama, Glamorama, and a score of ill-fated 3-D imitations of Milton Gunzberg's. The audience's eyes became adjusted to width, to the release from the frame the new Westerns and travelogues provided. Titles grew longer and longer, de-signed to fit into the entire width of the screen. *How to Marry a Millionaire, Bad Day at Black Rock, Love Is a Many-Splendored Thing, The Man in the Gray Flannel Suit, Love Me or Leave Me*: these were typical of the time. Glittering words spelled out in vulgar pinks or sequined blues an-nounced the awfulness of the entertainment to come: colors were fuzzy and washed out; close-ups horribly bloated and

Jack Warner testifying before the House Un-American Activities Committee in 1947. Behind him is Paul V. McNutt. Committee members include Richard M. Nixon *(second from right);* Chairman J. Parnell Thomas is to Nixon's right.

Eric Johnston and Louis B. Mayer listening to Jack Warner's 1947 testimony before HUAC.

Film stars fly home after protesting a Washington probe of alleged Communism in Hollywood in 1947. Included are *(left to right, in front)* Richard Conte, Lauren Bacall, Humphrey Bogart; *(behind them)* Paul Henreid, June Havoc, Geraldine Brooks; *(third row)* Marsha Hunt, Evelyn Keyes; *(behind Miss Hunt)* Jane Wyatt; *(lined up behind Miss Keyes)* Danny Kaye, Gene Kelly, Sterling Hayden.

The Hollywood Ten and lawyers arrive in Washington after indictment. *(First row, left to right)* Herbert Biberman, attorneys Martin Popper and Robert W. Kenny, Albert Maltz, Lester Cole; *(second row)* Dalton Trumbo, John Howard Lawson, Alvah Bessie, Samuel Ornitz; *(back row)* Ring Lardner, Jr., Edward Dmytryk, Adrian Scott.

Dore Schary poses in his office.

Harry Cohn with his wife *(right)* and Rita Hayworth.

Nicholas Schenck testifying before the Senate in 1941.

Spyros Skouras (*left*) with brothers Charles and George.

Three pioneers: Cecil B. DeMille, Sam Goldwyn, and Adolph Zuckor.

Joseph R. Vogel (*left*) receiving an award from the Italian government after the filming of *Ben Hur*.

Jack Warner *(with phone)* and associates viewing 3-D.

Darryl F. Zanuck and friend, Irina Demich, at the premier of *The Longest Day.*

Part of the scene at the MGM auction in 1970.

distorted; actors and actresses became giants and giantesses, a Lauren Bacall spread like some Brobdingnagian monstrosity from one end to the other of the giant screen, a lean-visaged Gregory Peck seemingly afflicted with mumps. Through a mauve and cinnamon world the characters moved in a stupefying succession of feather-brained sequences, though Jean Negulesco brought a degree of romantic charm to the evocation of Rome in *Three Coins in the Fountain* and to the musical *Daddy Long Legs,* and Henry King achieved some intensity in the passionate exchanges of *Love Is a Many-Splendored Thing.* Intimate dramas like *Love Me or Leave Me*—the story of the torch singer Ruth Etting and her affair with a gangster—seemed awkwardly applied to a wide screen, while the musical *There's No Business Like Show Business*—awash with garish color and offering typhoon Ethel Merman on six track stereophonic sound—was an abysmal spectacle. Only in a few films could a hint of Hollywood's former standards of craftsmanship be detected: in the firm playing of Richard Egan and Marjorie Rambeau in *The View from Pompey's Head,* in the sparkling fifteenth-century costumes of Walter Plunkett and the sets of Hans Peters for *Diane,* and in John Sturges' vibrant direction of the rustic conflicts of *Bad Day at Black Rock.* Occasionally, a striking image emerged: rain beating on a car roof in *The Bottom of the Bottle;* a journey up a scenic railway in *Love Is a Many-Splendored Thing;* an exquisite moment in *The Eddy Duchin Story* when a girl with a red umbrella takes a walk through Central Park in the rain; the journey of the wooden horse in *Helen of Troy.* Here and there, a director or a performer seemed to increase in stature with the width of the new screens. John Ford had never been as warmly at ease as in the glowing landscapes of *The Searchers,* shot magnificently in VistaVision by Winton Hoch; and in *Rebel Without a Cause* and in *Giant,* a James Dean could create a breadth and depth of characterization equal to the new ratios that established him in one short, brief stroke as a great actor.

If James Dean, moody, remote, defensive, hiding a bitter anguish behind a sudden flashing smile, seemed the quintessential early fifties male star, then Marilyn Monroe, launched along with CinemaScope as 20th Century-Fox's greatest asset, was the perfect female prototype. She, too, came from the America of yearnings, of inarticulate dreams and aspirations in a mechanical juggernaut society; she, too, seemed remote, spaced, lost, a haunted, dark spirit sheathed in an almost absurdly voluptuous body. Her obvious vulnerability, combined with an acting talent not noticed by a whole lip-smacking generation of American males, makes her performances today seem almost unbearably moving. She was the most gifted of amateurs, the most pitiful of the Golden Girls; her genius was as real as Chaplin's, and far more genuinely poignant. Dean, dead at twenty-four, Monroe—after, many believe, a disastrous involvement with a noted political figure—dead at thirty-six: it was almost too perfect an American pattern of obscurity, suffering, early success, overexploitation, and sudden death.

True, a film like *Marty* came along to prove that narrow, drab accounts of life in New York, shot in plainest black and white, might show up all the hollowness of wide-screen. But it would be churlish to deny the freedom and beauty of many of the new images, the engaging, stagy folly of such comedies as Frank Tashlin's *Will Success Spoil Rock Hunter?* and *The Girl Can't Help It*. The cinema often reverted back to the Broadway stiffness of the first talkies, but it had its modest, witty Broadway pleasures.

Unhappily, though, wide-screen did not as drastically improve the industry's fortunes as many believed. The ballyhoo and buildup, the yellow, blue, and purple streamers, only half concealed a persistent desperation. Attendance levels, it was true, rose to fifty million people in 1953, an increase of five million over the previous year, but this was scarcely enough to offset the gigantic increases in costs of the new equipment. Month after month, battles raged in Washington and New York courtrooms as the two national organizations of exhibitors, Allied States Association and the Theatre Owners of America, unsparingly attacked the new high rentals, charged that the majors still strove to drive independents out of business, and that various systems of arbitration were notably failing to work. Distributor against exhibitor, mogul against struggling small-time theater owners; it was a heartless, constant battle which did nothing to help a divided and unhappy industry.

More and more methods were found of circumventing the division of the chains from their owners. On one hand, Si H. Fabian and Samuel Rosen's Fabian Enterprises, which had bought the Warner chain, involved itself in Cinerama and obtained—despite grave objections from some exhibitors—the exclusive right to show the system. Later, they went too far: they tried to buy Warners, thus seeking to restore the situation before Warners lost its theaters. But on this occasion the Department of Justice firmly ruled out their bid. Paramount's divided chain merged with television, becoming part of the American Broadcasting Company as ABC–PT, and Walt Disney formed his own distribution organization, Buena Vista.

Television had started a move from New York to Hollywood that was to accelerate in the years to come. Eagle Lion Studios vanished and was turned over to television; Paramount converted the old Warner studios on Sunset Boulevard to KTLA at a cost of $2 million. Herbert J. Yates, head of Republic Studios, told an annual stockholders' meeting on April 7, 1953, that he intended selling his entire backlist of movies, something the other studios had been refusing to do for years. "I see a bigger profit market in films sold for television than pictures for theaters," he announced to his astonished board. In the meantime, closed-circuit TV showings on large-screen theatrical circuits were still popular, the Notre Dame Series football game of 1953 attracting half a million viewers in one night. Twentieth Century-Fox began an effective if short-lived policy of showing six minutes of scenes from forthcoming attractions on Ed Sullivan's CBS program.

The most important event of 1954–1955 was Howard Hughes' outright purchase of RKO-Radio Pictures after several years as a major shareholder for $23,439,478. "For the first time in history," wrote *Film Daily*, "one man was the sole owner of a major producing–distributing company."

A year later Hughes had grown impatient and sold the company at a small profit to the General Tire and Rubber Company for $25 million, while the entire inventory of 740 features and 1,100 shorts passed to C and C Super Corporation for $15,200,000, giving the purchaser sole rights to show the pictures on television. It was a major point of breakthrough: apart from Republic, no other major company had agreed to part with its film assets for the rival medium. But it left RKO denuded, with a severely reduced production lineup as well, and when Daniel T. O'Shea, a former RKO attorney and special legal adviser to David O. Selznick, took charge, he had a tottering palace to lord it over. Every cent it took to buy RKO was borrowed from the Chase Manhattan Bank, which would obviously foreclose if a new profitable sale could not be made or a satisfactory production lineup organized. O'Shea was unable to save the studio and finally it was knocked down with the Chase Manhattan's approval to Lucille Ball's and Desi Arnaz's television producing company, Desilu.

Another ailing studio was Warner Brothers, which had failed to compete with 20th Century-Fox by creating rival systems of WarnerScope and WarnerSuperScope and had been ignominiously forced to toe the Skouras line. Its ventures into CinemaScope, started late and hurriedly, did not have the overwhelming success hoped for, and the studio passed into the hands of the Boston banker Serge Semenenko. Mary Pickford, increasingly unhappy with the running of United Artists, sold her 25 percent interest, consisting of 4,000 shares, to the UA corporation. At Columbia, Harry Cohn still seemed overly confident; Universal ticked along at low pressure, observing a policy of caution; Paramount plunged its resources into VistaVision. But it was at MGM that the really dramatic things were happening in that artistically vapid decade.

The origins of the supercolossal struggle at Metro lay in the studio's disastrous post-1946 history under Nicholas Schenck.

Early in the 1950s the MGM stockholders began to become more and more restive, noticing the dwindling profits that resulted from his policy which clung to the romanticism of the past, the "nice," genteel vehicles for stars like Greer Garson or Mickey (Andy Hardy) Rooney. Schenck finally laid the blame at the feet of Louis B. Mayer, whom he had never really liked and whose personal flair and knack for obtaining publicity had cast him into shadow. When shareholders began to create a hubbub based on the studio's loss of several million dollars between 1947 and 1951, Mayer and Schenck appointed Dore Schary, recently dislodged as RKO's head of production by Howard Hughes, head of production, while Mayer acted in a supervisory capacity as studio head. Schary's first picture, *Battleground,* became a great success, infuriating Mayer, who had not been anxious to make it. Mutual jealousy between the two men was aggravated when Schary began referring directly to Schenck on matters of policy, bypassing Mayer entirely. When Schary followed *Battleground* with a series of flops, Schenck stood by him simply in order to annoy Mayer, of whom he had grown thoroughly tired. Whenever New York executives visited Hollywood, Mayer would buttonhole them and tell them Schenck was out to destroy him.

By 1956, MGM's losses were $4,600,000 in twelve months. Schary, whose lavish Esther Williams vehicle *Jupiter's Darling* lost $2,200,000 and the story of the Pilgrim fathers, *Plymouth Adventure,* lost $1,800,000, clearly had to go.

The trouble with both these films was that they were too heavy and solid for the masses, and too historically insubstantial to please the critics. "Taste," clearly, in the Eisenhower period, was the last thing the American public wanted. Consequently, Schary was fired, heading for Broadway to write inflated, liberal dramas like *Sunrise at Campobello* and a version of Morris West's *The Devil's Advocate,* while the power in Hollywood passed from Nicholas Schenck— pushed out as chairman of the board—to Arthur Loew, stolid son of Marcus Loew, who had founded the company and had died almost thirty years before.

Loew brought in the veteran Wall Street bankers Lazard Frères and Lehman Brothers to help prop up the company's shaky finances. But these firms became increasingly aggravated by MGM's foot-dragging policy, its inability to bring in sufficient fresh blood to a board severely overburdened with late middle-aged, old, or non-industry figures, including a well-known general. Loew, disliking his role as president, backed down after a year in office, after achieving nothing, and the new presidency went to a virtual nonentity, selected for his colorlessness and for his long experience in theaters: Joseph R. Vogel. He was a dull, nondescript, doggedly ambitious man, born in New York on September 7, 1895. Educated at Townsend Harris High School, he became a part-time theater usher, spending his nights studying accountancy until he obtained his goal—treasurer of the Loew's Theatre in New Rochelle and later of the Seventh Avenue Theater in New York. He moved from management of small theaters to that of the Loew's State in New York, biggest of the entire chain, in 1924. Ten years later, his plodding determination had earned him general managership of the entire Loew's out-of-town circuit. Eleven years after that he was head of all Loew's theaters and in 1948 he became a director.

As reserved and obscure as Schenck, Vogel was not a particularly likable man. But his competence, despite his ignorance of picture-making, seemed unassailable, and his modest realization that he had been chosen after numerous possible executives had refused the post won the grudging respect of many of the board, of which he was consistently afraid.

While he began to make plans, Vogel was already being threatened behind the scenes. Louis B. Mayer, largely inactive since his rather unsatisfactory period with Cinerama earlier in the 1950s, began to scheme for Vogel's downfall, not because he wanted the job himself, but because he wanted to see the MGM which had rejected him fractured and fissured. He strongly supported two men who were determined to overthrow Vogel and bring a new, aggressive leadership to MGM: Joseph Tomlinson, a tough Canadian contractor who already owned 5 percent of Loew's stock, and Stanley Meyer, an undistinguished, hustling producer of TV series, including Jack Webb's laconic *Dragnet*.

At a succession of executive meetings, Tomlinson, a rough-hewn, powerful man with a way of trouncing his adversaries that they often found terrifying, thundered brutally against Vogel's rule. Squabbles grew to the hysterical pitch of a Rod Serling teledrama, as other directors blew about like straws—this way with Tomlinson's chilly Canadian bluster, that way with Vogel's smooth New York calm. On March 21, 1957, Tomlinson issued a statement to the board condemning Vogel outright and demanding that Louis B. Mayer be given the presidency, with Stanley Meyer as vice president. Vogel detested these squabbles as much as Tomlinson enjoyed them, and he felt as much respect for the older members of the board, many of whom had served under Nicholas Schenck, as Tomlinson had not. Vogel dismissed all those executives who were opposed to him, leaving only four—and adding a further two who were in his support: American President Lines chief George L. Killion and former Secretary of the Army Frank Pace.

Finally, in the winter of 1956–1957, matters reached a head. In February a meeting was held between interested parties at Manhattan's Drake hotel, in which Joseph Vogel and his attorneys met with Tomlinson and Stanley Meyer and their own legal advisers. The Tomlinson–Meyer attorney, Ben Javits, told Joseph Vogel bluntly that unless he accepted a split board, made up half of Vogel's supporters, half of Tomlinson–Meyer's, powerful banker–shareholders would put the pressure on their fellows to have Vogel forced off the board. The bluff—and it was a bluff—worked. Vogel accepted this uncomfortable situation, and a thirteenth board member, Ogden Reid, the president of the New York *Herald-Tribune,* was added as a neutral to help preserve the peace.

Predictably, though, the two warring factions failed to hold hands, and every successive meeting that spring and summer was a painful ordeal for all concerned. Vogel divided his time between New York and California, not always attending board meetings, busying himself with widespread dismissals in Hollywood and with a close supervision of his new production chief, Benjamin Thau.

On July 12, Tomlinson and Meyer struck again. At a special Hollywood board meeting combined with an inspec-tion of the company's facilities, C. R. MacBride, representing the management consultants Robert Heller and Associates, who had been investigating the company for the past several weeks, stunned Vogel and his faction by saying that he had decided he wanted Vogel removed at once. Vogel challenged the statement, and weeks later Robert Heller and Associates climbed down. Meanwhile, Vogel decided to use everything in his power to oust Tomlinson and Meyer, once and for all, from the board.

Exhausted by the constant struggle, four directors backed out, and Vogel finally decided to bring the whole matter to a spectacular showdown in October.

The setting of this dramatic climax was Loew's State Theater, of which Joseph Vogel had once been a manager; 1,100 MGM shareholders streamed in to watch the new comedy, *Don't Go Near the Water,* designed to put them in a relaxed mood before they saw the real drama to follow. The struggle of the giants proceeded for ten hours and twenty minutes, as Tomlinson, bitterly furious, clashed with a cold and detached Vogel. "I don't want control of the company! I want good management! You cannot get it until the old guard is rooted out! You, Mr. Vogel, are not capable of rooting them out."

The reply was typically cool: "Are you through, Mr. Tomlinson? I want to give you every opportunity." As Vogel finished, a stockholder, thoroughly delighted, yelled, "Get the boxing gloves!"

The end of the meeting was a victory in Vogel's favor. By adding several more directors to his board, he secured a 13 to 6 majority, and his cold eloquence won over most of his stockholders. Vogel and Benjamin Thau rushed out announcements of their forthcoming projects: William Wyler would start production at once on a lavish new version of *Ben-Hur,* Yul Brynner and Maria Schell would appear in *The Brothers Karamazov,* Paul Newman and Elizabeth Taylor in *Cat on a Hot Tin Roof,* Frank Sinatra in *Some Came Running.* The backlist of MGM films would be leased —not sold—to TV, a wise move as it turned out, since MGM retained its magnificent library of movies and could re-release such classics as *Gone With the Wind* and *The Wizard of Oz* constantly and profitably. Even the distressed stockholders felt a little bullish as 1958 dawned. But their pleasure was to be short-lived, and Metro headed for still more treacherous waters as the next five years wore on.

10

In the wake of CinemaScope's enormous original success, Spyros Skouras had become (following Louis B. Mayer's virtual retirement) the major figure in the industry. But by the late 1950s, the novelty of wide-screen had worn off, and industry figures with good memories recalled that in 1933, six years after talkies began, another novelty had faded and movies had faced their worst crisis. It became painfully clear to Skouras that his inspired gimmick had only brought about a temporary relief, not a cure for the industry's ills. The directors of 20th Century-Fox put constant pressure on him to find some new device which would improve matters, and asked him to find methods of disciplining Marilyn Monroe, the studio's biggest asset, who was proving troublesome. By 1959 he had failed to find a solution to any of the problems facing him and his company. He paced around his mansion at Mamaroneck on Long Island Sound with its Greek retainers, Greek food, and Greek statues, knitting his brow in an agony of indecision.

It was at this particular moment—when his days as head of the company seemed to be numbered—that Skouras received an important long-distance telephone call from the producer Walter Wanger. Wanger, a suave and polished man, with a record of duplicity and skillful maneuvering in the industry, had edged his way to the post of head of production at Paramount Studios in the late 1920s, finally easing Jesse L. Lasky, the production chief who had befriended and hired him, out of a job. Later, Wanger himself had been dislodged and had moved from studio to studio as a smooth but shifty freelance with a string of box office pictures to his credit including *Queen Christina, Foreign Correspondent,* and *Smash-Up.*

He told Skouras he had a sensational idea which would "save" the studio and enable it to create a new *Gone With the Wind.* Skouras, an impressionable man for all his monolithic solidity, listened and agreed to see Wanger, who flew in next day from Hollywood, enthusiastically announcing that the subject was *Cleopatra,* starring Elizabeth Taylor. Even though the subject had been flogged to death in previous movies, and the last version, Gabriel Pascal's *Caesar and Cleopatra* (from Shaw) had flopped, Skouras incredibly thought the idea a good one. He went to a file and dragged out a faded copy of the script of J. Gordon Edwards' 1917 version with Theda Bara. The two men immediately signed an agreement to go ahead, and Skouras told his astonished board that he would personally stand or fall on the success of this new venture.

From the outset, *Cleopatra* became Skouras' obsession. "I couldn't sleep or eat thinking about it," he told me. Unfortunately, he did not receive support for his own idea of casting Elizabeth Taylor—the only logical choice if the picture was going to have any chance of international success.

Buddy Adler, vice president in charge of production in Hollywood—an irritable, cigar-smoking man mortally stricken with lung cancer—dismissed the idea and asked Skouras to consider Joan Collins. Skouras suggested Gina Lollobrigida or Sophia Loren. Wanger and Skouras finally went back to Elizabeth Taylor, but did not make her an offer, and Skouras told Wanger to make up a script geared to her personality.

Wanger engaged an actress with little or no writing experience, Ludi Claire, and a script clerk, Stanley Scheuer, to prepare a basic treatment, separately and unknown to each other; later, he handed Scheuer Miss Claire's work to rewrite. She caught Scheuer retyping some of her pages and stormed off the picture. The English novelist Nigel Balchin was called in. Skouras and Wanger floundered from writer to writer, never seeming to make the correct decision.

After a series of discussions and a reading of Balchin's first-draft script, Elizabeth Taylor—in London for the shooting of Joseph L. Mankiewicz' *Suddenly Last Summer*—finally agreed, after a series of refusals, to play the part, telephoning jokingly to ask a mere million dollars for her efforts. Skouras was horrified by the unprecedented demand and began talking about Susan Hayward, star of Wanger's last film, *I Want to Live,* for the role. On October 9, 1959, Wanger telephoned Miss Taylor, who was now staying at the Beverly Hills Hotel, and told her she had definitely been ruled out. She climbed down by $250,000 and on October 15, Skouras grumblingly signed her. Six days later, Skouras chose Rouben Mamoulian to direct, and Jack Hildyard to photograph.

A tall, elegant, fiercely proud Armenian, Mamoulian had made his name as a young man with celebrated stage productions (*Porgy, RUR*) on Broadway and some of the most daring and inventive early sound films (*Applause, Love Me Tonight*). His career had fizzled out in the 1940s following his unceremonious removal from *Laura* after a series of behind-the-scenes struggles with its producer, Otto Preminger. His flamboyant visual style, brilliantly expressed in the color effects of *Blood and Sand* and the bold blacks and whites of *The Mark of Zorro,* would seem to have been ideal for *Cleopatra,* and the studio was uniformly enthusiastic about his hiring.

In November, Skouras, now reluctantly convinced that *Cleopatra* should be a major production but still looking for ways to cut corners, was forced into a disastrous decision. He decided to make the film in England, where the Eady Plan he himself had worked out with the British government, making British government financial aid possible provided there was a percentage of British cast and crew, would substantially help to underwrite the costs of production. Elizabeth Taylor had to work in Europe for tax reasons and had that in her contract. Despite the fact that British weather was atrocious and the sunny atmosphere of Egypt could scarcely be evoked there, Wanger and Mamoulian actually flew to London to investigate facilities. They were horrified at the cramped conditions of Pinewood Studios and the drizzling gray skies of England.

Skouras talked of shifting the location to Turkey. The art director, John DeCuir, and a production manager flew to look at Istanbul before determining it would be impossible. Wanger hired Lawrence Durrell, whose perfumed novels showed no ability at dramatic construction, to revise Balchin's script. Mamoulian wanted to make the film in Italy, but Skouras finally returned to the idea of making the film in England. Wanger's May 19, 1960, diary entry reads: "This is absolute disaster. Hollywood has given us an August 15 starting date, but we don't have enough studio space, don't have full cast, don't have a script, and don't have a crew of laborers."

Skouras, in London that June, angrily rejected Wanger's and Mamoulian's complaints about the weather, and the fact that Balchin's script—even with Durrell's revisions—was unusable, but privately sympathized. On July 11, Production Chief Buddy Adler died suddenly of lung cancer in Hollywood. His death cleared the way to a more lavish budget, and Skouras made plans—at Mamoulian's insistence—to at least shoot some exteriors in Egypt. But the bulk of the picture was still to be shot at Pinewood, a cramped, totally inadequate studio outside London.

In August, 1960, Skouras saw to it that palm trees began arriving in Britain from Hollywood and Egypt. Under his advice, John DeCuir began building seven and a half acres of massive sets of Alexandria in drenching rain, using 142 miles of tubular steel, 20,000 cubic feet of timber, seven tons of nails and 300 gallons of paint to create temples and palaces. Later that autumn, Elizabeth Taylor, always in delicate health and only recently recovered from pneumonia, fell ill with influenza. At Skouras' desperate insistence and despite Wanger's and Mamoulian's pleas, shooting began in September, in forty-five-degree weather and a thin drizzle, with no satisfactory script, with a disaffected crew, a grumblingly miserable director, and, astonishingly, most of the other main roles not yet cast. By October 22 very little had been shot and Elizabeth was still unwell; the insurance company and the Chase Manhattan Bank wanted the picture closed down and the star immediately replaced. Worse still, fog descended on the lot making the sets and cast totally invisible. Dismissed from the hospital by her doctors, the star came down with an undignified boil on the buttocks, an infected tooth, and sundry other complications, culminating in meningitis, an inflammation of the membrane covering the brain.

In December, shooting was dragged on desultorily, with Elizabeth Taylor appearing on some days and not on others, and with Stephen Boyd as Mark Antony and the Australian actor Peter Finch as Caesar. Everyone by now hated the script, and the experienced Nunnally Johnson was called in for rewrites. Day after day, all concerned were locked in anguished quarrels, trying to find their way through a morass of production errors as thick as the fog outside the ill-heated sound stages. By January, Mamoulian had had enough. "It was impossible," he told me. "Nothing could be done to save that appalling dialogue we were handed day by day, and the terrible weather. The picture, needless to say, should never have *begun* in England."

Skouras' version was: "I made a terrible mistake in hiring that Armenian in the first place. He was once talented—but no more. The footage he shot in England was terrible. He can't blame the weather because the stuff he did was mainly interiors. He was out of the Lubitsch school and he did the whole thing like a comedy. It was obvious he didn't take the thing seriously at all, and I nearly dropped dead when I saw that horrible footage."

Fox had insured the picture with Lloyd's against production losses for $3 million, but Lloyd's—claiming gross incompetence and an improper choice of the shooting site—offered only $1,250,000. (The court finally made them settle for $2 million.) In a last-ditch effort to save a collapsing film, Skouras fired Mamoulian and hired Joseph L. Mankiewicz, writer–director of several Fox successes (including *All About Eve*). Mankiewicz was asked to abandon the projected *Alexandria Quartet* and rewrite the screenplay and direct the picture. By February, 1961, with production at a halt, Skouras realized the full horror of the fact that more than $10 million had been spent and that every foot of film previously shot would have to be scrapped. Incredibly—and despite the fact that the star was stricken with influenza again due to the severe climatic conditions—he again decided to recommence shooting at Pinewood, six months after it had been proven that shooting there was futile.

On March 4, Elizabeth Taylor came down with double pneumonia and was rushed to the hospital. Two nights later she was in a critical condition, her death widely reported and predicted by an eminent physician to take place within the hour. A tube in her windpipe to enable her to breathe, she hovered between life and death for hours. As she fought her way to recovery, all work on the film was again abandoned, and Elizabeth Taylor and her husband, Eddie Fisher, flew home to Hollywood.

In California the entire massive production was replanned from scratch. The scriptwriter Ranald MacDougall—notable for his witty screenplay for *Mildred Pierce*—was engaged to write an entirely new scenario. In April, Skouras decided the picture would be shot in Hollywood, with locations in Egypt, and some preliminary footage shot in Rome. (The entire picture could even more economically have been shot in California itself, but for the studio to have shown that degree of common sense would have been a miracle.) In the meantime, the sleepless Skouras was getting deeper and deeper into trouble: Representatives of Wall Street firms arrived on the Coast to check over the grievous financial situation in part caused by the *Cleopatra* extravagance; nobody there had complete autonomy, not even the studio's new nominal head, Peter Levathes. Months dragged on as Ranald MacDougall continued to work on the script. Finally, by late summer, it was decided, because of Hollywood labor costs, to make the entire film in Rome, abandoning MacDougall's script; Mankiewicz would instead improvise one from day to day.

In September the company arrived in Rome and immense sums were spent in remodeling an entire building to give Elizabeth Taylor a lavish five-room dressing area. She and her husband were presented with the fourteen-room, sumptuous Villa Papa at a rental of $3,000 a month. Finally, on September 25, shooting of the new production began with Rex Harrison as Caesar and Richard Burton as Mark Antony. But once more the results were disastrous: the rainy, icy weather was as severe as England's, the set of the Forum was flooded, much welcome but unflattering publicity attached to Elizabeth Taylor's affair with Richard Burton. No sooner had the company arrived in Italy than it was faced with a variety of lawsuits. Italiana Galatea Film Productions—which had originally been engaged to assist in the production as early as 1959—sued for $1 million damages because its preparatory work had not been used. The Italian Communist Party stimulated riots by disclosing that white and black dancers in the crowd scenes were housed in different dressing rooms. The circus owner Ennio Togni demanded $100,000 for "unused elephants" hired but never used for a royal procession. "The elephants are insulted," he said.

The *paparazzi* descended on Elizabeth Taylor with their customary ferocity, followed by an angry crowd which objected to her cleavage when she was accepting a local award. At Anzio, where a replica of Alexandria was being built, a bulldozer struck an unexploded shell and was blasted to pieces. An awkward incident took place when a group of congressmen visited the set at Cinecittà as the invited guests of the Italian Government. When it proved—after a three-hour wait—that Miss Taylor would not be pleased to see them, the aggrieved visitors told the press they were appalled. In turn, the congressmen were severely criticized by the press at home for spending public funds on visiting movie sets.

By November, *Cleopatra* was again in serious trouble. Torrential rain and savage winds made location shooting impossible. Spyros Skouras arrived in Rome and shrieked with rage at his executives, notably the agonized Wanger, but only a personal visit to heaven could have averted the weather problem. Production costs were by now so staggering that a $12,500,000 figure seemed the only logical ceiling anyone could put on the budget, and that was a quarter of what the film finally cost.

"Elizabeth Taylor added five million dollars to our budget

in Italy," Skouras says. "She tried to commit suicide four times because she believed Burton was losing interest in her and she wanted to frighten him. On one occasion she almost succeeded—if they hadn't left the car roof open on a drive to Rome from her villa she *would* have died."

By May, 1962, the monstrous production was still dragging its feet. Publicity was endless, much of it still concerning the continuing off-screen romance of Taylor and Burton, a field day for the columnists. Skouras sent Peter Levathes, head of the studio, to Rome. Levathes demanded that Wanger be taken off salary, and told Mankiewicz that the film must be finished no later than June 30. Wanger was horrified to learn that he was forbidden the right to cut the picture. But he proceeded anyway without payment, holding the studio to his contract and traveling to Egypt in July for the shooting of the final scenes. (Elizabeth Taylor wanted to join Burton there, but she had sold bonds for Israel and was refused a visa.)

In Egypt during these climactic weeks of shooting, some of the most serious problems of all occurred. Jews working on the picture had their mail opened and censored, and their telephone calls tapped. Wigs and makeup did not arrive, the transportation arrangements failed, costumes were misdirected, the heat proved unendurable. Wanger recorded in his diary for July 2, 1962: "We sleep under tents because of the bugs. There are scorpions in the locations and the sand gets into everything. We have no privacy."

Joseph Mankiewicz collapsed with exhaustion after several weeks of this. (Fortunately, Elizabeth Taylor had not been subjected to the rigors of the location.) Finally, on July 24, 1962, shooting ended. But the agony of *Cleopatra* was not yet over.

Budget estimates showed that the picture had cost $44 million, almost ruining the studio in the process. It was the end for Skouras. Shattered, he moved to the nominal post of chairman of the board, and Darryl F. Zanuck arrived from Paris to take over. "Darryl himself helped to crucify me," Skouras says.

Monstrous and misshapen and marred by its crassly vulgar central female performance, *Cleopatra* finally opened at the Rivoli Theatre in New York, and at the Pantages, Los Angeles, in June, 1963, four years after it had originally been prepared. An early plan to release the picture in two parts of three and a quarter hours each was abandoned by Darryl Zanuck, who personally supervised the final cut, removing many scenes and trimming others.

Newsweek remarked that the picture cost "more than half the endowment of Princeton University," and "exceeds the total expenditures of the United States Government during George Washington's administration. . . . Whether *Cleopatra* will turn out to be a monumental accident or an accidental monument remains to be seen." Skouras told the magazine, "The film cost at least $20 million more than it should have. I was the president then. I take the blame." *Newsweek* unfairly laid the blame firmly at the pretty feet of Miss Taylor herself: "Her illness, her romance [with Burton] and her fairy tale standard of living . . . Queen Elizabeth's $800-a-week hairdresser, her $50,000 a week, overtime pay, her $3-million-dollar flirtation with death." And Skouras was more justly chastised: "Skouras' desire to hurry [the picture] up, the incredible wastefulness of building sets before a script was finished, of shooting against the odds of the weather, and rushing pell-mell to completion, at least doubled the cost of the picture."

The critical reception for this farrago was on the whole absurdly warm. *The Hollywood Reporter* gushed in terms that would make anyone but a press agent blush: "Power and passion are the twin and intertwined themes of 'Cleopatra,' and they have never burned with greater intensity or amid such opulence as they do in this extraordinary film. . . . Miss

Taylor is the supreme star of the screen. Her beauty has never been more radiant." Bosley Crowther wrote in *The New York Times*: "A surpassing entertainment, one of the great epic films of our day. Elizabeth Taylor's Cleopatra is a woman of force and dignity, fired by a fierce ambition to conquer and rule the world." Rose Pelswick in *The Journal-American* wrote: "Miss Taylor, at her most beautiful, brings alive a Cleopatra of allure and ambition." The Burtons were better critics, failing to attend the premiere and remaining in England instead. In England, where pressure from advertisers was less severe, the film was often seen for the monstrosity it was.

Cosmic vulgarity was perfectly all right, but financial failure was not. Despite its endless publicity, *Cleopatra* was slow in getting off the ground. By mid-1964, the studio announced that it had not yet made half of the picture's production costs. In April it sued Elizabeth Taylor and Richard Burton for $50 million breach of contract. The suit specified that they "maliciously interfered" with the firm's property rights, and complained of "their conduct with each other although each was to the public's knowledge at these times married to another." She was accused of not appearing for work on time, not performing her duties properly, and of not appearing on set in a condition to be filmed. In turn, Elizabeth Taylor and her former husband Eddie Fisher sued the studio: they jointly owned 85 percent of the Swiss corporation MCL, which owned in its turn 35 percent of *Cleopatra*. She demanded that all prints of the film be placed in receivership as 20th Century-Fox had "mismanaged distribution of the film."

These suits were finally settled with a reasonable degree of amicability. But it was years before *Cleopatra* repaid its costs. *Newsweek* commented: "For love of her, Caesar gave his heart, Antony gave his life, and Twentieth Century-Fox a corporate treasure." And Spyros Skouras his professional life.

11

Following the great MGM proxy fight of 1957, the tensions at the studio were extreme. Louis B. Mayer's death from a blood disease on October 29 of that year was all too painfully symbolic of the decline of a studio that at any moment might be taken over by Wall Street and demolished for a real estate sale. Joseph Vogel was in constant collision with his board, and Benjamin Thau, on the Coast, was hard pressed trying to correct the problems resulting from Dore Schary's commercial failures.

Thau was a mild and reserved man with little liking for the enormous problems of running a studio and few certainties about ways in which to save it. He had been a loyal MGM servant, beginning in 1929 when he was transferred to the West Coast after working as an officer of Leow's theater booking division in New York. When the company started to make British productions in the 1930s, Thau was placed in charge of several of these, and he obtained a succession of distinguished foreign players as contract artists. Just before World War II, he became Mayer's personal assistant, and with Mayer and Eddie Mannix he ran the studio. In 1944 Thau became an executive vice-president, acting mainly as liaison for stars between Hollywood and New York.

Vogel hired him because of his immense experience with actors but from the outset the two men failed to see satisfactorily eye to eye. Their main difference was over the commitment of the studio to a new policy of sumptuous spectacle films typical of MGM's heyday under Mayer. Thau believed that a Mayer-ish policy of massive musicals and historical dramas would work triumphantly, while Vogel, all too sharply aware of the studio's parlous financial state, was terrified of the board and uneasy about putting through requests even for studio repairs.

Thau's impatience with Vogel, and Vogel's cowardly caution, resulted in a series of heated telephone squabbles between New York and Hollywood. Finally, Thau lost his constraint and decided to revive Schary's original plan for a lavish remake of *Ben-Hur,* one of the studio's major silent film successes. Thau immediately ordered an investigation of facilities at Cinecittà Studios in Rome, found out how to settle any local problems by the expected Italian bribery and corruption, and insisted Vogel supply $600,000 for the building in Italy of major sets.

Vogel refused, saying that the board would never tolerate such a figure. Thau insisted that Vogel look away while the sets continued building; and the board simply wasn't informed. By the time $600,000—and more—had been invested, the horrified board learned the truth. Vogel nervously informed its members that he had allowed Thau to commit upwards of $7 million—enough to imperil the studio itself—toward making the epic, and that Thau had hired the very expensive William Wyler to direct it.

Making the film involved a *Cleopatra*-like risk of the very existence of the studio itself, then at its lowest ebb. But Vogel, fired by Thau's enthusiasm, decided the gamble was worth it if only to prove the daring effectiveness of his threatened administration. And unlike the *Cleopatra* gamble, this one paid off.

In charge of the project was Sam Zimbalist, a charming outgoing—but ailing—man in his fifties who had begun his career as an office boy for the then president of Metro Studios, the late Richard Rowland, and became the stage manager of the silent screen star Nazimova. In 1923 he became an editor at MGM, cutting the early sound films *Alias Jimmy Valentine* and *Broadway Melody*. In the 1930s and 1940s he emerged as a producer (*Boom Town, Tortilla Flat*) and was known as an effective presenter of spectacle films (*King Solomon's Mines, Mogambo*).

Zimbalist had originally planned to make the picture in 1952, engaging Sidney Franklin (*The Good Earth, The Barretts of Wimpole Street*) to direct. He believed that Franklin's refined sensibility would be ideal for the subject. The production was shelved when Marlon Brando, the prospective star, refused to play in a religious subject, and when Schenck resigned and Schary and Eddie Mannix left the studio. Franklin went to England, and rejected suggestions that he might later direct the film (he was afraid his fragile health might not stand up to the ordeal).

General Lew Wallace's novel was first published in 1880, when Wallace was governor of the Territory of New Mexico. It sold 500,000 copies within eight years and by 1891 it had become even more successful than *Uncle Tom's Cabin*. Five million copies had been bought by the time the second film version appeared.

In 1907 a one-reel version was shot without permission of the author's estate. Sued by Wallace's publishers and executors, the film's makers claimed that they had simply provided an advertising puff for the book. The court awarded them $25,000.

In the 1920s a syndicate bought the rights to *Ben-Hur* and sold them to the Goldwyn Picture Corporation in return for half the gross ($3,050,000). Made by MGM, the first *Ben-Hur* was a spectacle marred by painful sentimentality—which the writers of the new version all too carefully preserved.

The complicated story had little to recommend it save the fact that it provided opportunities for scenes as lavish as the same studio's version of Henry Sienkiewicz's *Quo Vadis,* made several years earlier. (A Jew, Ben-Hur grows up with a Roman, Messala, and in time they become powerful enemies. Ben-Hur is sold into slavery, while Messala becomes a patrician. As a grand climax. the two men fight it out in a spectacular chariot race.)

Casting the major roles was a difficult process. Scores were ruled out—including Ann Blyth in the female lead—before Charlton Heston was chosen to play Ben-Hur and Stephen Boyd to play Messala. Wyler's discipline whipped them into a semblance of shape during rehearsal, but they still could do little with the painfully stilted dialogue.

A battery of scriptwriters was engaged to adapt the book, including Karl Tunberg, S. N. Behrman, Maxwell Anderson, Gore Vidal, and—finally—Christopher Fry, who was engaged specifically—and futilely—to increase the emotional temperature of the major dramatic scenes. Henry Henigson, gifted general manager of the project, spent more than a year in Rome assembling a million props; cameraman Robert Surtees and second unit director Andrew Marton left for Europe in the early spring of 1958; six hundred sets were being built. The press, in April and May, began printing elaborate accounts of the massive preparations: seventy-eight Lippizaner horses obtained in Yugoslavia, twelve North African camels transported across the Mediterranean, 750 workers engaged to build the stadium for the chariot race alone.

The chariot race arena covered eighteen acres and was the largest single set built up to that time. Two alleys of wood alongside the arena walls were 1,500 feet long; four massive statues of wrestlers towered thirty feet high. Nine chariots, taking fifteen months to build, were also prepared. In addition, two Roman galleys, each 175 feet long, were made fully seaworthy, two hundred artisans created a thousand suits of armor, and 10,000 other costumes were designed by Elizabeth Haffenden.

Shooting the chariot race was a major challenge for Andrew Marton, who directed it as head of second unit, for Sam Zimbalist, who supervised the brilliant cutting of the sequence, and for its cinematographer, Harold Wellman. In January, 1958, Marton and his team began looking for suitable teams of horses. Bought in Yugoslavia, they were shipped to Italy and carefully trained on an identical track.

Marton had a serious problem in finding a satisfactory surface for the track. Despite hard work in libraries in Rome and Hollywood, the MGM research team failed to turn up the necessary information. The track had to be firm enough so that the chariots did not skid or spill. It had to have a satisfactory drainage system and a sanded top to prevent the cement laming the horses. "We started with ground rock debris," Andrew Marton said later, "which had to be steam-rolled. That was covered with ten inches of ground lava, and *that* was covered with eight inches of crushed yellow rock."

The drivers began to train in February, led by Charlton Heston and Stephen Boyd. Heston's experience in Westerns made the driving of the chariots a comparatively easy matter, but Stephen Boyd's hands were torn to ribbons at the initial tryouts. For the scene in which Boyd was flung from his chariot and dragged in agony by the horses, he refused a stunt man and—protected by heavy padding—underwent the ordeal himself, emerging bruised and in fact permanently scarred.

Disaster was narrowly avoided in a scene when the camera car, moving in front of the chariots, suddenly stalled. Only the instinct of the Yugoslavian horses, which swerved away at the last minute, prevented the camera crew from being trampled to death. At another stage, the stunt man Joe Canutt, son of the special expert in such scenes Yakima Canutt, was catapulted into the air and down between the horses' hooves, dragged several feet, and almost killed.

Each portion of the race was carefully planned in advance. For ten weeks shooting continued with the most difficult shot of all kept to the end: when the chariots of Ben-Hur and Messala became interlocked.

Marton wrote, in *The American Cinematographer:* "In order to show the immediate danger in which they were, I decided to pan from the interlocking and splintering wheels to the two antagonists in vicious combat. To get this effect we had to chain the camera car to the two chariots. I didn't have time to realize that if one horse stumbled, the whole contraption—horses, chariots, stars, camera car—would crash and pile up in disaster."

Charlton Heston endured more than his usual variety of tortures for the role: kicked by the stallions he drove in the chariot race, walking under a searing sun for thirteen days, covered in rats in a galley scene, floating up to his neck for hours at a stretch in an icy Mediterranean. Stephen Boyd's eyes were severely infected by the use of contact lenses and production was stopped for three weeks while he recovered. A major row took place when manager Henry Henigson was infuriated by being excluded from a central spot in a crew photograph taken during shooting. Emissaries flew in from Hollywood to try to settle this and other trivial disputes. Then, in November, 1958, Sam Zimbalist, after working round-the-clock to cut the chariot race, felt an agonizing pain in his head and chest while sitting in his villa near Rome. He collapsed and died of a heart attack.

Zimbalist's death was not the only major problem that the studio was faced with. Another was the decline into serious illness of Henry Henigson. The new studio chief, Sol Siegel, realizing Henigson was ailing and deaf, had to dismiss his old friend over dinner in Rome, subtly recommending "a vacation in Switzerland." Henigson took the hint and left; he was replaced by Joseph J. Cohn, an experienced studio executive who had long worked with Mayer. Wyler's direction was extremely slow, and Siegel had to fight to keep expenses down. Wyler's habit of shooting every sequence from countless angles then selecting one in the cutting proved infuriating, and the MGM cutters, under Siegel's orders and very much against Wyler's wishes, reduced the film from five and a half hours to about three and a half.

By the outset of 1959, sixty-five reels with 1,500,000 feet of exposed film had been shipped back to Hollywood for processing. Vogel—who had already spent $15 million on the production and constantly quailed before the fury of the board—pressed on with the studio's most ambitious publicity campaign to date, masterminded by its skillful department head, Howard Strickling.

Vogel spared nothing on the campaign: $1,750,000 worth of advertising space was bought, ensuring excellent reviews in a number of newspapers. Libraries across the country showed special displays of stills. Dr. Joseph Mershand, president of the National Council of Teachers of English, prepared a special study guide for use in schools. Ben Stahl painted a sequence of pictures which traveled from specially hired gallery to gallery, and the cast was dragged through a lethal schedule of cross-country interviews. *Film Daily* alarmingly announced "More school children will see *Ben-Hur* than have seen any other motion picture ever made. MGM started months ago to focus school attention on *Ben-Hur*. They began this campaign with special emphasis on junior and senior high school, and figured this would be a mammoth market.

. . . However, it has been discovered that elementary schools are as keenly interested as the higher grades."

A telephone call to MGM was answered with the words, "Good morning, this is MGM, and Ben-Hur is coming"; one wit noted that Ben-His and Ben-Hur towels were being mass manufactured. Ben-Hur T-Shirts were in fact made by the scores of thousands; together with toy replicas of the galleys where Ben-Hur worked as a slave, plaster statuettes of Charlton Heston in a tunic, Ben-Hur swords for children to duel with, and sinister little chariots with spiked wheels.

The premiere at Loew's State in New York was devoid of ballyhoo, reflecting the conservative tastes of Joseph Vogel, who shrewdly allotted the best seats not to stars or other Hollywood visitors but to the bankers and investment brokers and their families instead. Bosley Crowther liked the film: "The most stirring and respectable of the Bible-fiction pictures ever made [and] vastly surpasses the silent version released in 1926." Archer Winsten of the *Post* unsagely observed: "The most realistic, the most literal rendering of ancient Roman, Judean and Christian history that can be imagined." And Ruth Waterbury of the *Los Angeles Examiner* not ironically said it was "jam-packed with inspiration." In Hollywood, the premiere at the Egyptian Theatre was more glamorous, with the Gary Coopers, Irene Dunne, Jimmy Durante, Audrey Hepburn, and George Montgomery and Dinah Shore arriving by searchlight glare.

In the wake of the film's release, an unpleasant situation occurred: William Wyler fought the Screen Writers' Guild ruling—following arbitration—that sole credit for the screenplay should be given to Karl Tunberg, protesting that Christopher Fry had contributed important material toward the script. (Why anyone should want credit for it at all seems far from clear.)

Another controversy arose when *The Christian Century* in November, 1959, inconveniently suggested that Protestants should challenge "the promotion of lurid distortions of the Bible," and that "Ben-Hur made other biblical epics look like pikers in this perverse translation which would replace art with gaudy but costly trivialities. . . . Protestants need not subsidize those vulgar efforts to use the Bible against itself."

Charlton Heston—in Boston for promotions—told Station WBZ: "I'm afraid *The Christian Century* has crawled out on a very narrow limb which will shortly precipitate them into an embarrassing quicksand," while Wyler told UPI, "There are no orgies and very little sex in the picture. There are only two kisses in the entire film. This is a story without a single bubble bath scene." And he added with more honesty than most, "It is not a biblical film." Asked by Richard Mason of *The New York Times* what he intended doing next, he said with a sigh, "A small romantic comedy."

Ben-Hur was, in financial terms, a triumphant vindication of Vogel's and Thau's colossal gamble, making by the time of its 35mm release (November, 1968) as much as $66 million. Moreover, Vogel pleased the stockholders by revealing that he had trimmed off $17 million in studio overhead during the past two years, more than justifying the $15 million spent on *Ben-Hur*.

Within a year, it was obvious that Vogel's and Thau's gamble had paid off, and that *Ben-Hur* was going to save the studio. News of its success excited Hollywood into a whirl of activity, and MGM into starting a whole new policy of major remakes of its successes of the past.

Urgently behind a blanket policy of remakes was Sol C. Siegel, who had replaced Benjamin Thau in 1959. Born in New York, Siegel came to Hollywood from a journalistic career in 1934, helped to form Republic Studios, and introduced Gene Autry to the screen. In 1940, he left Republic and took over his own unit at Paramount, where his *Perils of Pauline* and *Blue Skies* were handsome, successful, and tuneful. His commercial skill was later confirmed when he produced *High Society* (a remake of *The Philadelphia Story*) as a Bing Crosby/Grace Kelly/Frank Sinatra musical for Metro. He also worked at Fox, producing such successes as *A Letter to Three Wives* and *Three Coins in the Fountain.*

In 1956 he had been offered the presidency of Loew's Inc. but had turned it down. He was reluctant to accept the new job of production head, but Joseph Vogel talked him into it, offering him a salary of $300,000 a year.

Siegel's reign got off to a highly dramatic start. In mid-January, Siegel received a letter threatening his life and that of his wife, Ruth, unless $100,000 was paid immediately to a box number. The FBI unearthed the identity of the extortionist—a thirty-four-year-old commissary pantryman, Herbert Strauch. Arrested while making a threatening call to Siegel in a studio telephone booth, Strauch admitted he had seen the production chief's name in an advertisement of a current picture.

That momentarily unsettling experience was nothing compared to the horrors of making *Mutiny on the Bounty* in 1960–61, which resulted in the end of Siegel's reign at the studio and seriously affected his health. Originally, the concept seemed exciting—although those with good memories recalled that the prior version had not been an altogether overwhelming success at the box office. In 1959, Joseph Vogel told the shareholders, more amenable now because of the immediate strong reaction to *Ben-Hur,* that this new picture would be "more thrilling than the original mutiny itself." He should have added that it was going to be even less authentic than the 1935 version.

Teams of researchers in London and Hollywood began to prepare the background of the film. Siegel, in the grip of a romantic daydream, planned the rebuilding of a replica of the *Bounty,* to be sailed to the South Seas, authentic from its rope davits to 11,000 square feet of canvas on the square-rigged masts. Naturally, the Metro version had to be larger than the original: 118 feet as against 85 feet long, with a beam of 30 feet 6 inches, a 14-foot draft, with a tonnage of 480 gross and 128 net. The construction was supervised by James Haven, master of special effects, and Fred Ruhland.

The *Bounty* was the first three-masted schooner to have been built since the 1880s, and the first ship to be built from the keel up for a motion picture. The original blueprints in the British Museum were carefully followed, and when the ship was finished she was given a complete crew of twenty-three men, including a cook. Her sailing from Lunenberg, Nova Scotia, was a magnificent sight. Her 11,000 feet of canvas proudly unfurled and 1,000 people massed on the wharves as she set sail for a trial run twenty-nine miles out to sea under the splendidly named Captain Ellsworth Trask Coggins.

Unfortunately, though, costs of building the *Bounty* had risen high above the original expectations. Its construction budget amounted to $750,000, due to the fact that early winter weather had prevented the delivery of wood for the keel. Since it could not be brought across the heavy snowdrifts blanketing Nova Scotia, it had to be sent by sea from New Jersey, and the extra costs and delays were formidable.

At last, the *Bounty* set sail for Tahiti. But her voyage was dogged by problems. Her twin diesel engine caught fire, and her master was forced to send an S.O.S. to vessels which had just sailed past, offering their passengers the immense excitement of seeing a vision from the past. Immediate plans were made to abandon ship, but luckily James Havens managed to douse the fire. The extreme discomfort of sailing through heavy swells caused half the crew to go down with sea sickness. It was December 4, 1960, three months after her expected delivery, that the *Bounty* finally docked in Tahiti.

The film's star, Marlon Brando, cast as Fletcher Christian, was hired by the producer, Aaron Rosenberg, an ex-collegiate football star with a successful track record at Universal (*The Glenn Miller Story*). Brando was offered a number of directors whose names he impatiently rejected, finally settling on Sir Carol Reed, known in the trade as a "four walls" director, though he had made *The Outcast of the Islands*. The script went through several hands, and a lengthy writers' strike delayed work on it unconscionably; finally it was tackled by Charles Lederer, an uninteresting writer whose chief claim to fame was as the nephew of Marion Davies. Trevor Howard and Richard Harris were added to the cast, and the company and crew, headed by Rosenberg and Reed, finally arrived in Tahiti in 1960 with an incomplete script, and production preparation as inadequate as that for *Cleopatra*.

From the outset, the project was doomed. Carol Reed's gentlemanly cool upset Brando, who also quarreled with Richard Harris, and, infuriatingly, continued from day to day rewriting the script and attempting to tell Reed how to direct. After a few weeks, Reed was stricken with gallstones and flew back to Hollywood for an operation. He told Siegel, "I don't really think this is my cup of tea. Take me off it."

Siegel felt a change of director would have been a mistake, and asked Reed to return to Tahiti, himself flying out twice to try to soothe everyone's ruffled brows. Reed, though, proved immensely slow, too painstaking for such an immense budget, and after an agonizing month Rosenberg appealed to Siegel to fire him. Reluctantly, Siegel agreed.

Siegel than made a decision he later regretted. He engaged Lewis Milestone, a director then past his peak, to take over. (Brando had failed to approve anyone else, but liked Milestone's pacifist films *All Quiet on the Western Front* and *A Walk in the Sun*.) Milestone and Brando collided also, and frequently Milestone abandoned the direction entirely, simply falling asleep on the set or pleading illness while the crew, under cinematographer Robert Surtees, took over.

Weeks dragged by, and finally the rainy season forced the company to return to Hollywood, where the quarrels grew more intense. Simultaneously, disaffection increased among the studio heads, with Joseph Vogel in New York aggravating Siegel beyond endurance with news of the board's complaints.

Back in Tahiti again, the agony of *Mutiny* seemed endlessly protracted. Money hard-earned by *Ben-Hur* was spectacularly squandered on such items as flying Brando *The New York Times* at $27.94 a week, while the Bounty's insurance cost a total of $175,000 and the ship hired to check on the *Bounty* for insurance purposes cost $500 a day to run. Arthur Knight, who visited the location for *Show Business Illustrated,* wrote: "Actors complained that there was no shade, no place to sit on the *Bounty's* narrow decks. Grips complained that the actors perpetually got in their way as they snaked cables, rolled lights, or lugged the heavy camera from one end of the boat to the other."

Back in Hollywood, Marlon Brando decided to rewrite the Pitcairn Island scenes, showing himself sitting in a cave while the other mutineers looted and raped. Rosenberg was furious and threw the script pages in Brando's face. As a result, Brando failed entirely to act in the final five weeks of shooting; $2 million worth of film had subsequently to be scrapped. Later, he relented, and the scenes were reshot in Hollywood, but Milestone refused to direct them. Brando took over the direction himself, with the aid of the cameraman Robert Surtees. "It was eerie," Richard Harris told *The Saturday Evening Post.* "Like seeing a ghost ship with no one at the helm."

Finally, in 1961, the labor was over. *Bounty* cost $30 million, twice the most extravagant estimate of the budget. Many liked the film when it was first previewed, but it was in fact a disaster, relieved only by Carol Reed's sequence of the arrival of the *Bounty* and the presenting of the breadfruit.

Arthur Knight wrote, "Will this help or hurt?" It hurt. *Mutiny on the Bounty* was a $30 million disaster, wiping out many of the gains made by *Ben-Hur*. Aaron Rosenberg, chiefly by giving interviews from coast to coast where it counted, saved his professional neck, but few others emerged unscathed from that embarrassing fiasco. And it proved, like *Cleopatra*, a huge lesson: first, you need a script.

12

The blockbuster disasters proved only that pre-planning in Hollywood where millions of dollars were concerned was an essential of survival. Producers sat around Beverly Hills fires on chilly winter nights and told their families harrowing cautionary tales of vast movies entered into without satisfactory scripts, of stars and directors given unbridled freedom in their contracts, a freedom they flagrantly and greedily misused. Already, the old studio system, economically run, with pictures tailored to current economic conditions, with temperamental artists firmly refused permission to squander time and money, had burst apart. The lust for power of all concerned, and the unnerving habit Hollywood executives had of eating each other alive (not excluding their young), while preserving a sunny, crewcut image of golf-playing regular guys, were gaining more and more unwelcome comment in the world press.

Skouras ruining 20th Century-Fox through his unreasonable executive decisions on *Cleopatra* and Vogel and Siegel at constant odds at MGM were reported by magazines and newspapers sadistically enjoying the twitchings of the dinosaurs.

Yet during the harrowing years of success and failure, when a feeling grew that living in Hollywood was like playing Russian roulette every morning at breakfast, much else had been happening that was overshadowed by the spectacular events at Metro and 20th Century-Fox.

By 1960, total annual product had sunk from 500 to 200. Moreover, the industry had finally capitulated to television. This meant not merely launching the extensive production of series in Hollywood itself, but selling or leasing every single old movie in its vaults (except the sacred *Gone With the Wind*) for showing on the box. The efforts at wide-screen production had, as we have seen, very mixed results. Stars formerly prohibited from appearing on the little screen now frequently graced or disgraced it with their presence. Even the films of the fifties—uncomfortably, even hideously squeezed down from CinemaScope proportions—began to be shown only a handful of years after they were made, their color distortions made even less palatable by means of high-frequency transmission. Lucille Ball in the late fifties obtained control of RKO through her television production company, Desilu, and Red Skelton ruled the old Chaplin studios.

It was beside the point that television—by 1960 well past its Golden Age—was a horror; harsh in its turnovers and its pressures, its standards dictated by advertisers or ad agency executives, its punchlines relentless and its distortions of the great traditions of the American film, from knockabout farce to Westerns and melodrama, beneath contempt. The monster had to be fed, and Hollywood had held out with ridicule too long. Now gifted directors, their creative talent wrecked through the vanishing of confidence, the old studio system and guaranteed audiences, emerged directing soap operas or medical-crises dramas with one ailment cured per week, while a new group of talented men who came up in the great days of live TV—men like Sidney Lumet, John Frankenheimer, Ralph Nelson, Franklin Schaffner, George Roy Hill, and Arthur Penn—understandably preferred to work in feature films. Low, even medium budget pictures, in which so much of the best work in the history of Hollywood had been done, vanished seemingly for good. On the larger scale, alongside the blockbusters, many films of smaller ambition but greater quality had been seen: Billy Wilder's witty *The Apartment,* a comedy about office workers in New York; Joseph Mankiewicz's *Suddenly Last Summer,* with Katharine Hepburn and Elizabeth Taylor going elegantly insane in New Orleans; *Sons and Lovers,* beautifully directed in England by Jack Cardiff for the ill-fated, energetic producer Jerry Wald; Robert Rossen's *The Hustler,* about pool sharks, with Paul Newman's most acute performance before *Hud;* Alfred Hitchcock's *Psycho;* and *Splendor in the Grass,* Elia Kazan's portrait—from a William Inge screenplay—of life in small-town America in the twenties. More typical of the early years of the new decade were cheerfully inane films, devoid of the hardbitten wit of the thirties or the gloriously abandoned kitsch of the forties, films of the caliber of *The Pleasure of His Company, Fanny, Breakfast at Tiffany's, Pepe, On the Double, Where the Boys Are,* or *Romanoff and Juliet.* Tissues of witless compromise, these were Broadway-style, empty-headed farragos, designed relentlessly to drag the middle-aged commutor from the box. (Jerry Lewis's inspired comedy *The Nutty Professor* was a witty exception to the rule.) Even these movies were frequently preferable to *King of Kings,* in which the late Jeffrey Hunter appeared as a Christ with shaven armpits, or a *West Side Story* with a simpering hero (Richard Beymer) and a maddeningly synthetic view of New York relieved only by patches of choreography from Jerome

Robbins. So poor was the general situation in 1960 that Elizabeth Taylor won an Oscar for *Butterfield 8,* a film she quite properly deplored, and so many lamentable epics were made that they achieved the overall title "spear and sandals" from their aggrieved critics.

Perhaps the most significant event of that period was the significant rise of the Independent Film Importers and Distributors of America, and the emergence of a host of independents, using the studios merely as distribution outlets. Simultaneously, too, censorship began to crack at the seams, a whole series of state-wide test cases causing considerable problems to the Motion Picture Code Administrator, Geoffrey Shurlock. By the end of 1961, the terms of the Code's Section Six, indicating that "sexual perversion or any inference of it is forbidden," were beginning to be ignored, and pornographic films were being shown in first-run theaters on both coasts.

On the one hand the MPAA was condemned for weakening its demands for following the Code; on the other it was praised for permitting very great freedom on the screen. Censorship was attacked by almost all informed critics, and the industry put the matter before the Supreme Court, which ruled in 1961 by a 5–4 judges' decision that states and municipalities must require a film to be viewed by censors prior to its public showing. The test case arose because the Times Film Corporation refused to submit *Don Juan,* a sexy screen version of Mozart's *Don Giovanni,* to the Chicago censors. The case was taken before the Court. An extraordinary number of public figures placed their power behind the subsequent unsuccessful appeal: it was a highly significant event.

Later, smarting at widespread criticism, the Chicago authorities no longer permitted policemen to censor films and tried to arrange for censorship to fall under general Illinois legislature. Pressure groups threw this scheme out and enforced a new system whereby a review board of six was appointed, and an appeals board was instituted as well. The first board was appointed by the police commissioner (though it did not include members of the force) and the second by the mayor.

Classification, too, became a major issue in 1961–62. Otto Preminger, in a heated television debate with Dore Schary, recalled the censorship battle over his film *The Moon Is Blue* when he called for "self-classification and self-censorship" on the part of all producers. The exhibitor Michael Woolfson suggested in 1961 that voluntary classification should be submitted to the MPAA for consideration, but the MPAA refused. Harry Brandt, president of the Independent Theatre Owners' Association and the American Congress of Exhibitors, turned down self-classification also, claiming that the producers had no right to decide what children should see.

More and more states, faced with the first trickle of an eventually engulfing tide of pornography, panicked and tightened up their censorship regulations enormously. In Abilene, Texas, religious circles brought about a measure which provided for banning and classification of the most rigid kind. It charged with malfeasance any parent or theater employee who admitted a minor without a parent or guardian to a censorable film. When the Tower Twin-Oaks Drive-In at Abilene played *Never on Sunday* without enforcing the rule, the exhibitors were prosecuted. The theater owner, Kathryn Jacob, fought gallantly against her persecutors and emerged victorious: the ordinance was amended to read that censors could only recommend, not enforce, the posting of classifications outside a theater. Later that year Mrs. Jacob was seized and charged with having shown the locally banned *Not Tonight, Honey,* but the case was thrown out of court.

Censorship grew more repressive in 1962. A new storm blew up over the film *The Connection.* The motion picture division of the New York State Education Department forbade the film a license, as its use of a four-letter word for heroin was regarded as obscene. It opened without a license at the D. W. Griffith Theatre, and the censor stopped all showings after the second day with a Supreme Court injunction. Finally the Supreme Court ruled that the word was not obscene and the film continued. In Georgia (reported William Specht of *Film Daily*) a small company, K. Gordon Murray Productions, refused to submit two of its films, *Wasted Lives* and *The Birth of Twins,* to censorship at all. Finally, the Supreme Court of Georgia declared that censorship in Georgia was "unconstitutional."

Together with the battles for censorship, due to be resolved in Hollywood's favor as more and more permissiveness swept the country and a squalid decadence began to characterize the average theater exhibit, 1960–62 had another point of conflict: the subject of runaway production. For years, with fewer and fewer features being made, the unions had been feeling a sense of desperation, all too conscious that many members faced the breadline. Now their own featherbedding and excessive demands for payment had fissured the structure of the labor–management situation in Hollywood. It became clear that the small greed of union members was pulling against the larger greed of the moguls; and even more that the people of Hollywood were not as concerned as they once had been to pull together for the overall good of the industry, but wanted slice after slice of a rapidly crumbling pie. While the unions moaned, the moguls simply shifted one picture after another to European locations, where labor was cheaper and crews could be kept to a minimum.

By proudly pricing themselves out of work, innumerable Hollywood technicians, ranging from inspired cinematographer to lowliest grip, rendered their own situation desperate for most of the decade. Of the older ones, those who were able to do so very sensibly retired; those who could not, turned to commercials; the younger ones did television or industrial films; only the very greatest—men like Leon Shamroy, Ted

McCord, and James Wong Howe—worked continuously.

Sam Spiegel was perhaps the most important producer to have announced, very calmly but definitely in the late fifties, that he was leaving Hollywood for good, and he believed the future of picture-making lay in Europe. Attacked by union leaders, he made *The Bridge on the River Kwai* in Ceylon, *Lawrence of Arabia* in the Middle East, and even *Suddenly Last Summer* in Britain. The dreadful *My Geisha* was shot in Japan; *Come September* and *Sodom and Gomorrah,* in Rome; *Goodbye Again* in Paris; *Once a Thief* in Madrid; *One, Two, Three* in Berlin; and *The Counterfeit Traitor* in Sweden. Such mammoth films as *Exodus* were located on their actual settings.

Actually, the runaway habit was more of an epidemic without much logic in its basis. Carl Foreman's *The Guns of Navarone* proved enormously costly because it involved transportation of military equipment across immense stretches of unfamiliar territory, and stars had to be put up in an immensely costly temporary accommodation. The most absurd example of runaway production was *Lolita.*

The director, Stanley Kubrick, made it in England because of the Eady Plan, a scheme whereby sums levied on every seat sold were returned to producers prepared to use a majority of British personnel. The result of the location was that the film was virtually ruined: it simply failed to evoke the seedy, jazzy quality of small American towns and the jostling, aggressive horror of the freeways that give the book its special atmosphere and fascination. Too often a picture that could have been far better and more conveniently made in virtually rainless states like Arizona or California was subjected to a constant battery of adverse weather, language and labor problems in Europe.

While more and more directors began to make their pictures away from Hollywood, the invasion of the European sensibility began in earnest, cracking wide open the self-contained provincial complacency of Hollywood, and similarly stripping it of its vulgar but likable confidence. For years Hollywood people had avoided reading all but the weekly or daily trade papers and had stayed away from foreign screenings; now they ordered translations of certain French critics and began seeing French movies.

Sometime in the fifties, press agents, doggedly collecting everything about their famous clients, began to discover that even the most humdrum craftsman—Otto Preminger, say, or a slick director of farce like Frank Tashlin—was being discussed in metaphysical terms in France, that the only thing Hollywood money could not buy (intellectual respectability) had suddenly been conferred upon it by—of all people—the Paris intelligentsia. At first, the tendency was to dismiss the French critics as "longhairs," but before long a delicious spectacle occurred: young French writers plunged their savings into Greyhound bus treks across America, arriving to sit at the feet of bewildered idols like Leo McCarey, a commonplace director of comedies and soap opera, or gruff old veterans used to shooting off the cuff like Hawks and Ford. Smart Jewish businessmen were at first shocked, then grudgingly pleased to hear themselves described as dazzling artists when pre-hippie longhairs arrived at their homes with battered 16mm prints of movies the directors themselves had utterly forgotten. Leo McCarey listened to the questions of two visitors from Paris for six hours, ferreting in his failing memory for hopefully self-flattering replies, and after the visitors at last left turned to publicist Don Prince with only one word: "Christ!"

Yet, only a few years after they had become half-welcome, half-ridiculous apostles of a new faith, these ragabones had become famous directors, a Truffaut, a Godard, a Chabrol, or a Rohmer emerging from the pages of *Cahiers du Cinéma* to present their visions to the world. Their homages to Hitchcock, Preminger, Nicholas Ray, and other idols continued for a decade, self-conscious, incorrigibly adolescent, still redolent of the peculiarly tiresome atmosphere of the magazine that gave them professional birth.

Their influence struck deep into Hollywood. In the first place, Hollywood directors, formal, accomplished, used to composing sequences with hair-trigger precision, started to abandon the academic composition, throwing away skills it had taken half a century to build up. Hollywood films, in the wake of such inflated home movies as Godard's *Breathless*, began to have a casual, unrehearsed look, a beginner's unease; camerawork fell off, color standards declined, and an overall slipshod slackness crept into Hollywood films. Welcomed as a revolution, the French New Wave in fact did nothing more than help wash away the exquisite skills of the great Hollywood professionals, replacing it with a pervasive and maddening amateurism.

But the final effects of this change were not to be felt for some seven years. Their immediate results lay in the superficial Europeanization of Hollywood and of its major figures, just as the journey to Europe resulted in the final and fatal dissolution of the tight structure of the Hollywood industry. Now directors dropped titles like *Jules et Jim* at Hollywood dinner parties, and laced their conversations with French, while producers allowed wives, aunts, and cousins to pad their expenses and freeload outrageously, with a total contempt for budget limitations, while visiting Europe. Sometimes a man would even buy a second house in secrecy in Switzerland, or salt away "extraordinary general expenses" in convenient bank accounts in Switzerland. Whole colonies of tax exiles settled in Switzerland, led by William Holden, Paulette Goddard, and Charles Chaplin several years earlier.

An age of fatal European influences, censorship battles, the rise of the mindless behemoth of television, runaway productions, and an increasing anxiety, a fissuring of Factory Town: the early sixties was an era of far from quiet desperation. In that harrowing period, perhaps only one group of Hollywood people really flourished: the agents. Able to charge a million dollars a star, breaking the hold the studios had over their clients in the form of long-term contracts, bartering and badgering and bleeding the producers, they emerged as major powers in the years to come.

13

The most powerful of the Hollywood agents was the tentacular Music Corporation of America. Through its influence, combined with the egotistical compulsions of the stars themselves, the great personalities, whose sexual magnetism provoked the world's dreams, gradually broke with the studios in the 1960s and set the pattern of so-called independent production which still prevails today. "I couldn't make *Casablanca* now," Hal Wallis told me in 1965. "The stars who could play the roles would cost a total of $15 million before we started." And, later, Hitchcock told me that he was horrified to discover that Julie Andrews and Paul Newman together cost him $2.5 million for appearing in *Torn Curtain,* leaving him insufficient money to make the picture. Encouraged by their agents, many stars began to choose their own properties, often without the wisdom once shown by their resented studio chiefs.

MCA began in 1924, when a Chicago oculist, Dr. Julian Caesar Stein, sank $1,000 of his savings into a two-room office and, together with a fellow collegiate, Billy Goodheart, formed a tiny agency. Born in 1896, Stein was the son of a struggling storekeeper, who became an eye doctor after unsuccessful efforts as musician and would-be aviator. He continued to play in bands in Chicago during and after his undergraduate years. He took up agency work when he found that no satisfactory agents existed to handle band players in the Midwest.

He was fortunate in rising at a time when night clubs were booming in Chicago, when stars like Paul Whiteman, Art Hickman, and Helen Morgan were spectacularly successful. He sold hotels on the idea of using not just one band as a steady attraction, but several, pleasing the customers by providing constant variety, filling his agency's coffers handsomely at the same time.

In the 1930s and 1940s, MCA developed its activities still further. Not merely did it book shows for hotels, it delivered a complete musical ensemble to a radio station or hotel.

Moving to Hollywood from its offices in New York, MCA set out to compete with the dominant William Morris Agency and with such important independent agents as Myron (brother of David) Selznick. MCA had the advantage of being able, through the sheer determination of some of its chiefs, to strong-arm tough bosses like Jack Warner and Harry Cohn into giving their clients better salary deals. Word of mouth did the rest.

David G. Wittels recounted in *The Saturday Evening Post* that MCA was handling between $40 and $50 million worth of clients a year, with some stars like Frank Sinatra earning as much as $1 million. That same year (1946) MCA was handling one-third of the stars of Hollywood, and Wittels pointed out that, of the several award winners or nominees in *The Lost Weekend* in 1945, all save Ray Milland were MCA clients. Betty Grable, Joan Crawford, and Bette Davis were among the many Jules Stein contractees. When the Hayward–Deverich Agency was dissolved in the late 1940s, Stein took it over. On Leland Hayward's and Nat Deverich's extraordinary list of clients were Ginger Rogers, Greta Garbo, Gene Tierney, Dame May Whitty, Joseph Cotten, Boris Karloff, Fredric March, Oscar Levant, and—among dozens of famous writers—Ben Hecht, Dashiell Hammett, and Dorothy Parker. Wittels maintained that the Hayward merger gave MCA more than seven hundred stars, handled from Stein's sumptuous offices in Burton Way, Beverly Hills, entitled MCA Square. "Inside," Wittels wrote in 1946, "are rare old English panelling, furniture and porcelain . . . a fabulous cut-glass English chandelier, reportedly worth $50,000, which is left lit at night to make a landmark of the place." The building also housed thirty offices for the staff, a radio station, a theater, a movie projection room, and a push-button, swing-out cocktail bar.

In 1946, Stein ceded the presidency to the thirty-three-year-old Lew Wasserman, a former theater usher and night club press agent whom Stein admired for his financial acumen and his ability to deal with stars. A hard worker, pallid, with piercing, melancholy eyes, Wasserman remained obscure and anonymous, protected like Stein by the giant intricate labyrinth which he commanded, dressed always in sober black. He insisted that his employees be equally reserved in dress and demeanor. Wasserman worked long days, and according to *Time* magazine (January 1, 1965), "limits phone calls to 30 seconds, will not read a memo of more than two paragraphs."

Stein and Wasserman together made a formidable team, beating the studios at their own game of wheeling and dealing, while being admired for their avuncular or paternal qualities by their client stars. One key to their success was their extreme parsimony. Despite the lavishness of their quarters, they were exceptionally careful with budgets and earned a reputation for turning profits on inexpensive films.

In 1947–50 many of the studios began to panic at the rise of television, drastically reducing their overheads by canceling the contract players who had been with them since the thirties. Some stars left voluntarily, already annoyed at being forced into films they did not want to make and being denied all participation in the profits. Directors and writers, too, drifted away, their contracts not renewed. MCA cleverly began to snap up one star after another, absorbing NBC and CBS contract players as well when government action prevented networks from agenting stars to themselves. MCA found themselves in an awkward situation once they had taken on a large roster of stars: how could work be found for them? In order to meet the problem, they launched into the packaging deals they had used in the hotel and night club business in the thirties. The agency made it clear to the studios that if they wanted a specific major star they must also engage another MCA client to appear with him, and, what was more, an MCA director, writer, and other accompanying players. Thus frequent examples of mismatching of actors occurred. The studios were held firmly over a barrel, and— because of the parlous state of the industry—the Screen Actors' Guild, which enfranchised agencies, had to concur when MCA took a further step and set up Revue Productions, a substantial TV film series manufacturing outfit, to provide a flow of work for its clients. Normally the SAG forbade an organization like MCA owning an outlet of this kind, but it provided year-to-year waivers for the time being.

In addition, MCA took a lease on Republic, and in 1960 moved in still further by buying Universal from Decca Records. TV programs, movies packaged by MCA, a whole studio devoted to MCA stars: it was a monopolistic situation that infuriated Attorney General Robert Kennedy and moves were made to start criminal proceedings against MCA.

Simultaneously, the Screen Actors' Guild threatened to give a year's notice to MCA to desist in its practices or it would be driven from the industry.

In Los Angeles representatives of the government conferred for months with representatives of MCA. Washington was anxious to avoid spending public moneys on the immensely expensive litigation that would result from any court action, and was happy to apply gentle but definite pressure on MCA to make a consent decree whereby it divested itself either of its agency or of its production outfits. After a good deal of tense arguing, Wasserman and Stein and their confreres settled on dropping the agency. This, says MCA/Universal executive Taft Schreiber, was chiefly because no film-producing company was rich enough to buy the production outfit.

In the wake of the severance decree, Stein and Wasserman, remaining chairman and president respectively, with Milton Rachmil (formerly of Decca) as vice chairman, concentrated all their intelligence on developing Universal from a manufacturer of cheapies to a front-rank studio, with TV production increased beyond any other studio's in Hollywood, and a roster of stars, directors, and producers who could be used in television or film interchangeably. Films could also conveniently be used in either medium. Under the effective guidance of Taft Schreiber, Stein's first employee back in the 1920s, Universal's television operation became the most efficient in Hollywood, with a policy of producing two-hour films for television. Edward Muhl conducted the film production side of the business with great effectiveness, preserving through its talent program the only remaining replica of an old-fashioned studio star system, giving stars or directors twelve weeks leave a year.

In 1962, MCA began construction of the glittering black tower which became one of Hollywood's most famous landmarks. Driving south from San Francisco, the first thing one saw, after winding through camel-hump hills north of the city, was the massive new tombstone of black spandulite, glass, and steel, 190 feet high, and not far beyond it the set of the *Psycho* house. The tower stood at the heart of a vast industrial complex including a bank, a hotel, and the largest backlot in Hollywood, spreading over hundreds of acres to the raw hills above Lankershim Boulevard. There was a charming rumor in the mid-1960s that the interior walls of the great tower were mounted on casters and moved by janitors at night, when the offices were deserted. The walls were closed in if you were out of favor and expanded outward if you were in. (If you found yourself in something resembling a telephone booth, you could start looking in the want ads.) The studio's production, *Mirage,* conveyed something of the flavor; and going into the tower and ascending in an elevator of prickly looking steel gave the visitor the feeling of being trapped in a safe, with the door locked from the outside. At lunch in the commissary, with everyone in funereal dark gray, the feeling was one of being in attendance at an interment.

But, despite its apparently gloomy air, Universal in the late 1960s began to gain in strength—achieving, chiefly through the activities of Ross Hunter, master of smooth soap operas, some major successes. Hunter's most important film, *Airport,* in fact grossed $80 million in domestic revenues alone.

MCA's nearest rival as an agency was William Morris. Morris, too, packaged, but it never made the mistake of buying a studio and a television production agency.

William Morris, Sr., was born Wilhelm Moses in 1873 in Austria. His father's fortune had been wiped out when he endorsed a note for a younger brother. The boy and his mother peddled needles and assorted knickknacks from a wheelbarrow, finally saving enough to travel steerage to America. With almost no English, Morris, in his teens, got a job on a clothing trade newspaper. In the stock market panic of 1894, the publication folded, throwing Morris out of work.

Morris applied to various theatrical agencies trying to obtain work (he had been successful at selling advertising space to struggling theatrical groups). George Lyman, the then leading variety agent in New York, was impressed by Morris and offered him a salary of $8.00 a week. Morris said, "Nine dollars or nothing," and was engaged. Lyman threw him a list of clients and told him to arrange bookings for them immediately. Morris doubled their usual fees. He also became a leading specialist in assembling vaudeville acts in packages for theaters. He began booking big, specially composed acts all over the country, acts consisting entirely of his boss's clients.

When Lyman died in 1898, his widow fired Morris, who bought the office with his savings and posted his own name on the door. When motion pictures came in, Morris saw their possibilities and went to the newly formed Biograph Company to obtain rights to show films. An anti-Semitic employee showed him the door. He took up distribution for Vitagraph instead, combining film showings with vaudeville bookings. By the twenties, he had built the country's largest single agency handling vaudeville acts. Finally he retired and was replaced by William Morris, Jr., a gentle, scholarly man who did not enjoy the agency business and left it for a teaching career.

Instead of William Morris, Jr., the new head of the agency was the diminutive, immensely charming and lively Abe Lastfogel. Born in 1898, son of a poverty-stricken, kosher butcher, Lastfogel went to work for Morris at the age of fourteen and became president within a few years. He is still head of the agency. Lastfogel established the California and Chicago offices and was largely responsible for building the company to its present eminence. Some of his vaudeville clients, including Jimmy Durante and George Jessel, are still with him. He moved into the film business with clients like Al Jolson and Eddie Cantor, typical of the many vaudevillians he handled at the dawn of the talkies. Almost certainly the most likable and brilliant agent in Hollywood's history, Lastfogel was a colossus by World War II, with Jules Stein at MCA his only serious competitor. During the war Lastfogel became head of the USO, arranging the appearances of entertainers for the armed services.

With his wife, the charming former vaudeville artist Frances Arms, Lastfogel continued to be an enormously popular Hollywood figure after the war. He built up his business as a packager with miraculous speed, beginning by packaging radio shows, later by packaging for network television. Among his clients were Sophia Loren, David Lean, Deborah Kerr, Kim Novak, Natalie Wood, Gregory Peck, Jack Lemmon, Steve McQueen (now with CMA), Fred Zinnemann, Elia Kazan, Garson Kanin, and Blake Edwards. He handled plays (Broadway and stock), magazines and books, concerts, fairs, night clubs, and merchandising of various kinds.

In the 1960s and 1970s Lastfogel and his staff developed film and television packaging deals with immense flair. As an example, the agency organized the deal for *Bonnie and Clyde* with Warner Brothers and *Love Story* with Paramount. William Morris's client, Warren Beatty, obsessed with the idea of making a film of the lives of Bonnie Parvier and Clyde Barrow (he had even commissioned a script), was combined with another Morris client, director Arthur Penn, and sold as a package to a reluctant Warner Brothers. Erich Segal, also a client of Morris, wrote the screenplay of *Love Story*; the Morris people encouraged him to develop it as a novel, launching that enormously successful book at just the right psychological moment when the public was saturated with pornography. The package—including the producer, William Morris client Howard Minsky, and the writer—was delivered to Paramount, and the wife of its production chief, Ali MacGraw, seized on it as a starring vehicle, partly due to a long-standing friendship with Segal. The rest is box office history.

Other agencies are legion, ranging all the way from glorified call-boy or call-girl services to bona-fide companies handling many distinguished MCA castoffs. Slightly outside the general run of agencies, dealing mainly in literary properties, is the tiny Irving Lazar, known in the trade as "Swifty," a former MCA employee who could beat any of his former bosses at the wheeling and dealing game. In March, 1966, *Newsweek* reported, of the properties he sold, a mere handful included *In Cold Blood* ($500,000 plus one-third of the profits), *How to Succeed in Business Without Really Trying* ($1 million), *The Sound of Music* and *Camelot* (both $4 million). Based largely on a Sammy Glick-like line of rapid talk, Lazar could argue anybody into almost anything—a fact that was proved when he convinced Warners they should make the disastrous *Youngblood Hawke*. But he could not outtalk the judge when in 1966 he was indicted for second-degree assault after cutting Otto Preminger over the eye with a bottle in New York's "21."

Another colorful figure is Kurt Frings, once representative of Elizabeth Taylor, who appeared in a slander suit in 1967 accused of abusing and threatening the interior decorator Helen Partello, with whom he had been conducting a stormy courtship. That same year he also figured in a legal investigation into the Friars Club in Los Angeles, where he gave testimony that he had been cheated at gambling.

Less newsworthy, more quiet and skilled, Paul Kohner was formerly in charge of foreign-language versions of movies for Carl Laemmle, the studio boss of Universal at the dawn of sound. When Laemmle disposed of Universal in the thirties, Kohner worked for a time at MGM, but he was not happy there. Asked how he started in the agency business, he said, "I found out that Joe Pasternak, producing at Universal, wanted to make a Deanna Durbin picture—he'd made her famous in the 1930's. I went to a friend, the writer Konrad Bercovici, and asked him if he had a Deanna Durbin subject.

He did. Then I went back to Pasternak and said I could get him a story for $50,000. He agreed. Bercovici usually got $25,000. Bercovici became my first client, and I was in the agency business with $5,000." Kohner acquired a valuable list of clients in subsequent years, including George Segal, Lana Turner, Maurice Chevalier, Ingrid Bergman, and John Huston—as well as lavish offices on Sunset Boulevard.

Today an agency is likely to be involved in packaging for television and film, and the agencies as a whole may be said to have been the prime movers in the "new" Hollywood. A network begins by approaching an agent and asking him if a certain star would be interested in appearing in a television series. The agency then finds a property appealing to that client—preferably a novel, play, or original story written by another client. The agency also finds a producer from among its clients. Gradually the elements begin to meld into a whole. The network is offered a combined property jointly owned by the creative participants. If the network is agreeable, then business discussions can commence. The agency simply takes 10 percent of the sale of the package as a fee, waiving its right to its usual 10 percent commission. A client—a Danny Thomas, say, or a Dick Van Dyke—given a package deal can often be in a television show for five years or longer and can become immensely wealthy as a result. A packaging studio is thus directly in competition with an agency. A studio preparing a show for television charges a sales fee (10 percent of the sales figure) but in addition has a very large overhead fee, intended as a method of redistributing back to the studio some of the profits from the show before the participants receive their funds. This fee can accelerate from 15 to even 30 percent. Agencies rent studio facilities for the package presentations and the charges are met by the joint owners of the show. An agency tries to make the production cheaper than the studio would be able to manage if it presented the show itself. The network buys the show outright and then has to find a sponsor.

When an agency packages for film, it takes, not 10 percent off the top, but merely 10 percent of each client included in the package. The studio meets the cost of production and guarantees distribution.

No stars today are in the million-dollar bracket. Up to four years ago, a few stars could obtain upwards of a million and a quarter dollars a picture plus as much as 50 percent of the gross. When the Hollywood "crash" occurred in 1969 and several studios, most notably Paramount and Fox, were overburdened with massive inventories of product costing $100 million, the studios bluntly told the agencies that stars who once were accustomed to receiving $500,000 or over would now have to settle for $200,000 or less. The day of gigantic salaries was over, not merely due to the failure of million-dollar-star vehicles but because the nervous banks now charged exorbitant interest rates, from 8 percent to 10 percent. (If a million dollars were to be advanced to a star, $100,000 interest had to be paid.) The economics of stardom had become absurd: a number of stars settled for less than $100,000 a picture, or in some cases nothing at all, taking instead a percentage of gross receipts. As a picture began to earn money, a star earned money "off the top" as well; the theory was that, even before a picture went into profit, a star would have realized his normal price. (Profits are usually obtained after a picture has recouped a minimum of twice its negative cost.) Even if a picture failed to "break even" it could still give the star a handsome return.

Contrary to the popular view, the studios still held a monopolistic control of the main lines of distribution; they were in 1971 as indispensable as they had ever been. Their salesmen, many of them twenty-five or thirty years in the business, knew the specific areas and the buyers intimately and were on a back-slapping basis with everyone who counted in a particular area. Films of one studio were often booked as continually into one theater as they were before severances occurred. Even when producers entirely outside the industry financed and presented a picture, the same distributors would be offered the film. Free-lance distributors have largely failed to equal the skill in selling of the majors. It is virtually impossible for an independent to succeed in selling directly to one of the regional chains, a fact that aggravates some agents who would like to sell directly to chains, bypassing the usual lines of distribution entirely.

TV Guide's Dick Hobson summed up (April 12, 1969) a typical life among agents: "He drives up to his client's house at four in the morning because the actor's wife has left him after eight years of marriage and three children . . . bails a series regular out of jail . . . keeps a fading leading lady out of sight until her face-lift bruises disappear . . . picks up his client's laundry . . . finds an abortionist for the girl friend of a TV series lead."

Agents tend to follow a pattern, a style of living, that has barely changed. Joe Hyams wrote in *Cosmopolitan* (October, 1969): "You see today's young agents tooling around Hollywood at all hours of the day in their black, air-conditioned, leased by the Corporation Cadillacs, hands tightly gripping the wheel, sunglasses-shielded eyes staring straight ahead." Hyams pointed out that agency men were handsome, their hair neatly razor-cut, in dark suits and black shoes, smoking a pack and a half of cigarettes a day and equipped with one ulcer per man. They talked in "mills" and "thous," seldom swore, and spent eighteen hours a day making smooth deals. Top agents would be likely to fly a private plane, ski at Sun Valley, occupy a home in Beverly Hills, and earn upwards of $50,000 a year. Walnut desks and discreet oak panelling were common, lamps were fluted and carried dark crimson shades, carpets deep green or beige. It was a muffled, suave, briar-pipe world these figures lived in, a white slave market in well-upholstered leather.

Many former agents became Hollywood producers, among them Peter Thomas, Jerry Adler, Ingo (brother of Otto)

Preminger, and Lester Linsk. Typical of the transition were Red Hershon and Sidney Beckerman, who formerly handled writers like Clifford Odets and Evan Hunter, and later co-produced *Marlowe* and *Heaven with a Gun* at Metro. Others even became heads of studios: Martin Baum of General Artists becoming boss of ABC Films after successfully packaging *Charly* and *The Killing of Sister George*, Ted Ashley of Ashley–Famous becoming head of Warners.

Despite highlighted examples like Ashley and Baum, Bernard Wolfe in *The New York Times* (June 18, 1967) ran a distinctly unflattering article on the agency business. Wolfe recalled an episode at a Writers' Guild banquet in the ballroom of the Century Plaza in the spring of that year. Created by Hollywood writers, a film was shown entitled *The Hidden World of Agents,* which showed "spiders trapping and eating caterpillars, maggots swarming over a fetid carcass, preying mantises spearing bottleflies." A voice-over commentary announced in the glowing terms of a James A. Fitzpatrick travelog: "The Hollywood agent is an industrious sort . . . in his plush office . . . making his daily rounds . . . welcoming clients with open arms at contract renewal time. . . ." Among agents mentioned were Freddie Fields, tweed-jacketed and bespectacled head of Creative Management Associates, his then employee Henry Willson, the creator of male stars, Ted Ashley, and Meyer Mishkin of the Mishkin Agency. "Festively," Wolfe wrote, "in gala plumage, Hollywood was eating its own." And Wolfe precisely evoked the reality of the situation when he showed that the finger-pointing writers were, however much they might dislike it, willing hosts to their parasites. "Underpinning the mass vilification, and feeding it, is a withering dependency."

In a world where human beings were bartered, bought, and bargained over, only those with the sharpest teeth could survive. Yet many damaged their own businesses in the late 1960s by the very pitilessness of their methods. They succeeded in pricing stars so high that companies preferred to try cheaper and newer players. By 1970 established stars were grumbling at agents who often refused to let them take parts for small sums plus percentages of the gross. It seemed to many commentators that some unwise agents would talk themselves out of existence—in the actors' market at least. But the packaging side of their activity showed no signs of flagging as the new decade began.

14

The 1960s were years of major upheaval, in which the very structure of Hollywood was permanently altered. Harry Cohn and Louis B. Mayer were dead and Nicholas Schenck retired (he died in 1969). Barney Balaban continued doggedly at the head of Paramount, though even he was forced to move from president to chairman in 1963, following directly on Spyros Skouras's similar move at 20th Century-Fox. Darryl Zanuck—firmly at the reins following the success of his D-Day movie *The Longest Day*—ran 20th from New York with his son Richard in charge on the Coast; Columbia, with Leo Jaffe at its head, was an efficient operation, Mike Frankovich in charge of production in California before he became an independent producer. Universal continued to thrive after the MCA Agency severance under its production chief Edward Muhl; Warners merged first with Seven Arts, a Canadian TV-production outfit, later with Kinney

(parking lots, janitorial services) and Jack Warner, ignominiously ordered to the back of the room at Seven Arts
board meetings when he proved vociferous, finally sold out
and entered theatrical and independent motion picture
production, still vigorously energetic in his seventies.

The years of the decade continued to offer the public a
spectacle of fabulous monsters gambling their lives away:
the commercial graph rose and fell as alarmingly as before.
Banks, chain grocery owners, oil interests, began to buy more
and more shares, offering handsome purchase sums to disaffected or distressed shareholders. Dividends were not always
paid: in the very late 1960s and early 1970s, MGM and 20th
were two firms which failed to pay a dividend at all. A *Sound
of Music* could be followed by the major flop of a *Star!* and
the profits of a whole line of moderately successful films
could be wiped out at one stroke. And the escalating union
costs, the massive, largely obsolete equipment, the cumbersome overhead-ridden character of the studios themselves
and the constant mismanagement made film-making an increasingly agonizing burden.

Public interest was focused on Paramount and MGM in
particular during the decade, for these studios were the
scenes of major takeover bids, indicating more than anything
else the dissaffection that existed on company boards, the
tensions with which all executives lived. In 1965, Paramount
had been through a rocky period: Barney Balaban, whose
background in theaters (the Balaban and Katz chain) and
almost thirty years as president made him deeply admired in
the industry as a whole, had failed to weather the storms
of that time. Quiet, reserved, cautious, he pursued a policy
of stringent economy and even traveled coach class on airplanes. Many unfairly blamed him for the Studio's failure
to use CinemaScope, falsely claiming that economic con-
siderations had made him avoid it. Many studio executives
felt that his caution and thrift were symptoms of advancing

old age; they were happy when he moved over to the nominal role of chairman, with Adolph Zukor, then in his nineties and the founder of Paramount, as chairman emeritus.

It was in 1965 that two energetic and pushing figures began to be particularly loud in their criticism at Paramount board meetings. George Weltner, president following Balaban, was forced in the spring of that year to admit to the board two men who jointly owned 8.75 percent or 135,000 shares of Paramount's common stock: Ernest Martin, a partner in the Broadway production outfit of Cy Feuer, and Herbert Siegel, whose Baldwin–Montrose Chemical Company owned a majority shareholding in General Artists Corporation, an important talent agency. Reminding him of the anti-trust action against MCA earlier in the decade, Weltner insisted Siegel divest himself of his GAC interests within a reasonable period of time. Siegel agreed, as president and director of GAC, and Baldwin–Montrose's board announced an intention to divest itself of GAC entirely.

By August, 1965, nothing had happened and Weltner became aggravated by Siegel's slowness in fulfilling his pledge. He apparently believed that Siegel and Martin were acting as conspirators in a plan to foist their clients on Paramount and were intending to use Paramount contacts to further their own ends, as well as planning to take over the company in a proxy fight. Actually, Siegel and Martin were genuine in their motive, which was simply to increase the fortunes of the company. They continually appeared at board meetings in New York, attacking current policy and—by a process of explicitly rude exposés of company weaknesses— seeking wholesale improvements. Weltner told reporters he was being faced with "harassment, insult and demoralization," and was only compelled to endure his suffering by virtue of the fact that Siegel and Martin were important shareholders. He also claimed that the two directors were leaking confidential information to their theatrical and agency contacts, which could be used against Paramount's interests in future client negotiations.

Matters reached a head in August, when Weltner, after a particularly stormy session, removed the two dissidents from the board on the ground that Siegel still owned GAC, and that Siegel and Martin had refused to countenance the regular quarterly dividend paid to Paramount shareholders from the company's inception. Martin's removal was justified by the assertion that his interest in Paramount had been financed by Siegel through the Baldwin–Montrose outfit.

Not content with his drastic action, Weltner now charged his enemies with violation of anti-trust statutes and demanded an open trial. He also arranged for friendly parties to snap up 300,000 shares, outweighing Siegel–Martin's package three to one. Among those aiding Weltner were Lehman Brothers, headed by Paul Manheim (on the Paramount board), Hallgarten and Co., headed by Maurice Newton, and William R. Forman's Cinerama.

In October the case successfully sought by Weltner had a preliminary hearing before Judge Edmund L. Palmieri at the Federal District Court in New York. Palmieri arranged a pro-tem agreement pending a further hearing whereby company board meetings would be held temporarily without the presence of Siegel and Martin. Siegel and Martin would approve any stock deal but would not have to approve film-making arrangements and both sides would be given ample opportunity to make depositions by December 3. In the same month, State Supreme Court Justice Joseph A. Brust ordered that Siegel should rapidly proceed to divest himself of GAC stocks. Louis Nizer, attorney for Paramount, scathingly described Martin at both hearings as "a mere pawn" of Siegel. Edward Bennett Williams, counsel for the insurgents, charged that Paramount was following a policy of attrition against men with multi-million-dollar investments and genuine deep interests in the company.

On December 6 the trial went ahead as planned, despite Siegel's claim that he had in fact begun to divest himself of GAC shares. Weltner was determined to oust him and his partner permanently and force them both to sell their shares.

Surprisingly, Edward Bennett Williams did not call for an immediate dismissal on the ground that his clients had answered Paramount's charges by going ahead with the GAC sale. Paramount's assistant studio chief Bernard Donnenfeld pointed out that such firms as the William Morris Agency would be unwilling to do business with Paramount so long as GAC had an interest in it. He said that similar representations had been made by Ted Ashley of Ashley–Famous, Richard Shepherd of Creative Management, and other important agents.

Cross-examining Donnenfeld, Edward Bennett Williams succeeded in making him admit that talent agencies acted only in an advisory capacity to their clients, that the Paramount–GAC relationship "provided no more of a conflict than a representation by Ashley–Famous of Paramount's subsidiary Plautus." Milton Rubin, attorney for Frank Sinatra, testified that his client would not deal with a company which had attracted bad publicity, due to its dissident members, and caused laughter in court when, referring to Paramount, he said, "If you pass up a girl because she's got a crooked nose, it doesn't matter if she's also cross-eyed."

The case closed in a flurry of rhetoric from Louis Nizer and Edward Williams. Nizer again charged that the circumstances of the GAC divestiture were "suspicious" and demanded angrily that an injunction be entered to prevent Siegel from re-acquiring his shares. "The court," he added, "is not required to believe Siegel's statement that he will immediately dispose of GAC shares."

Williams replied, "Louis Nizer's attack on the deal is haggling, piddling pettifoggery—it is remoteness squared to suppose that my client will undo what he has done." Judge Palmieri severely asked Nizer, "Do you want me to grant a prophylactic injunction to take care of all future evils?" "That's exactly what I am requesting," Nizer snapped back. And Nizer added a devastating point: that anti-trust laws were retroactive; since Siegel–Martin had been in breach, the only way they could satisfy the law was to resign forthwith.

Swamped with papers and documents several feet high, Palmieri closed the case without a decision, declaring that he would spend Christmas and New Year vacation weighing the evidence. The fact was that Louis Nizer had utterly failed to prove that GAC and Siegel–Martin were not parting company.

The case, decided by Palmieri in January, resulted in a victory for Siegel and Martin. Palmieri ruled that Siegel's General Artists Corporation was never in competition with Paramount, nor was Martin's Broadway production outfit. The judge further ruled that Martin was not acting improperly as Siegel's aide in various deals involving actors, and he had been satisfied that Siegel had disposed of General Artists shares as a gesture. He summed up: "The directors other than Siegel became disenchanted with the marriage of convenience hammered out in May. Siegel and Martin became *personae non gratae* to the other directors who felt that the tranquility of the Paramount board was being disrupted by the two newly elected directors." Immediately, the triumphant pair started plans for a proxy fight by demanding a complete list of all Paramount shareholders. In March they also insisted, at a hearing in the New York Supreme Court, upon seeing all the corporation's financial records. In March they informed the Securities and Exchange Commission that they would seek proxies against the company's present management at the May 23 annual shareholders meeting.

Suddenly their efforts were brought to an abrupt halt. On

March 24, as part of Weltner's carefully prearranged plan, Charles Bluhdorn, thirty-nine-year-old chairman of Gulf and Western Industries, came onto the board and offered Siegel and Martin $83 for each of their shares, or $9.50 a share higher than the closing price of $73.50 on the previous week's New York Stock Exchange. Surprisingly, Siegel and Martin accepted and left (approximately one and a half million dollars richer) while Bluhdorn's gigantic purchase made him the most powerful single shareholder on the board. It was only one step to his becoming chairman, and assuming absolute control of the company. Thus, by avoiding a proxy war, Paramount for the first time in its history lost its autonomy and became the possession of another company.

In May, 1966, a charged Paramount stockholders' meeting was held at the Americana Hotel in New York, attended by ninety-three-year-old Adolph Zukor, who had started the company in 1912. 1,295,056 shares were voted in favor of the merger with Gulf and Western, well over the two-thirds majority required for arrangements to proceed. Each outstanding share of Paramount common stock was converted by arrangement to 1.458 shares of Gulf and Western common, .0389 share of Series B. $3.50 Cumulative Convertible Preferred, and .21 share of the new G and W $5.75 Sinking Fund Cumulative Preferred Stock. Variety commented, "The film company's acquisition will provide G and W with a base in the field of leisure time activities, their reason for seeking the merger."

George Weltner pointed out in his speech to the stockholders that "Adolph Zukor was here at the beginning and he's here at the end," a remark that in itself enclosed an entire history. At the end of Weltner's speech outlining Zukor's career, the shareholders stood and cheered Zukor to the echo. Zukor smiled and puffed quietly at his cigar.

A few dissenting shareholders proved extremely vocal,

complaining bitterly about Gulf and Western's own shaky financial structure—and one man, John Campbell Henry, even heckled Weltner, interrupting his speech. He was told to be quiet or leave the room. Morton M. Adler, owning 2,200 shares, asked for a full investigation of Gulf and Western's books, while Sidney Siler, with only five shares, said, "I am worried that the creative art form that Paramount represents will be sold out to a larger holding company. I believe that, substantially, you don't make out a good enough case for having this merger go through."

Many believed that Gulf and Western was using the Paramount assets to buy a company called New Jersey Zinc. But the vast number of shareholders, depressed by Paramount's decline, felt they were better off with Gulf and Western than they were with the studio. They were pleased to get $90 for shares then valued at $75. Only 5 percent sold their securities for cash rather than accept G and W stock.

On the whole, the change was warmly welcomed in the trade papers. Later that year, in November, Howard W. Koch left his post as vice-president in charge of West Coast production, and ceded it to Robert Evans, who had recently been appointed head of European production. Koch became an independent producer—a role he had formerly occupied—starting with *The Odd Couple* in 1967. In 1967, Weltner retired, aggravated by the pressures accompanying his troubled reign.

By 1967, Paramount was being firmly run by Evans, a former garment-jungle tycoon and actor. Featured in *The Best of Everything* and *The Sun Also Rises,* he had begun acting in films, curiously enough, playing Irving Thalberg in *The Man of a Thousand Faces.* He was aided by Peter Bart, a *New York Times* West Coast correspondent who had written an interview with Evans at a time when it was of great value to Evans' career. Meanwhile, another major boardroom fight blew up at MGM.

In 1963, Joseph R. Vogel had become chairman of MGM, to be replaced as president by Robert H. O'Brien, a more effective administrator. Two months later, Vogel was removed as chairman. At the annual stockholders' meeting, Vogel was blamed for the studio's earnings plunging from $12,600,000 in 1961 to a mere $2,589,000 in 1963. *Mutiny on the Bounty* had become Vogel's *Cleopatra*: it destroyed his career as surely as the Egyptian epic ruined Skouras's. *Variety* headlined Vogel's enforced demise with characteristic cool: "Hero Today, Gone Tomorrow." Shattered, Vogel retired permanently to Palm Beach. He died of heart failure in 1969.

Few were saddened by his departure from MGM, least of all Benjamin Thau and Sol Siegel, with whom he had so bitterly battled. His triumph of *Ben-Hur* was forgotten; so, too, his success with *How the West Was Won*. People recalled only his fiascos: the $10 million lost on *Bounty,* the catastrophe of the $7,800,000 *Four Horsemen of the Apocalypse,* and $2 million spent on a production of *Lady L* that never materialized (a later version was made after Vogel retired, but it failed anyway).

O'Brien was a very different fish from Joseph Vogel. He rose through a first-class administrative career in finance, worked for many years with the Securities and Exchange Commission as an attorney, and later as an assistant to the president of Paramount, finally becoming treasurer of ABC-PT Theatres before joining MGM as treasurer and vice-president in 1957.

His career at MGM was a thoroughly successful one. Soft-spoken, quietly composed, he was a complete contrast with the cold, bad-tempered Vogel. When in office he immediately took, not a course of caution as many predicted, but a vigorous new plunge, gambling $12 million on a production of *Dr. Zhivago,* directed by David Lean. Bearing in mind Vogel's and Siegel's previous blunders, he insisted on a complete shooting script and plan of filming in advance; luckily, Lean preferred this kind of discipline, and the picture was an immense success, making more than $40 million and confirming the shareholders' faith in O'Brien. O'Brien also went ahead with commitments for *2001: A Space Odyssey*, and *Grand Prix*. O'Brien's brilliant record also included *Blow-Up, The Fearless Vampire Killers,* and the beautiful (though not commercially successful) *Far from the Madding Crowd*. Literate and intelligent, O'Brien may be said to have been chiefly responsible for all these worthwhile ventures.

Among the few not admiring of O'Brien was Philip J. Levin, a brusque New Jersey real estate executive, who bought 14.3 percent of MGM shares (720,000, purchased for $11,480,000) and, in 1967, decided to launch a Siegel–Martin-like onslaught on the board aided by nine other shareholders and Rosalind Russell, who intended running for an MGM directorship. Criticism assumed the fierceness of a boardroom struggle in MGM's own *Executive Suite* as Levin attacked O'Brien's outsize executive directors' fees. An anonymous Wall Street banker told *Los Angeles Times* correspondent Arelo Sederberg: "The fees are way out of line. Members of the MGM executive committee get $20,000. The chairman gets $30,000, the vice-president, $25,000. And for that what do they do? They say 'Yes.'" Levin charged that MGM was borrowing millions of dollars instead of using internal funds, and that its profits sprang from television production and the sale of features to TV.

In February, 1967, the MGM proxy fight took place at the same Loew's State Theatre where the previous battle had been staged ten years earlier. O'Brien's group came into the arena with 40 percent of the outstanding shares, and Levin with 34 percent. Addressing the 1,200 assembled shareholders calmly, O'Brien pointed effectively to the record of increased profits since he had taken office, and showed a handsomely made twenty-five-minute film illustrating important work in progress.

Levin walked up to take his place. Impassioned but preserving a calm exterior, he said: "At first I did not intend seeking a proxy fight. I simply felt that . . . I had a right to shape MGM's policy. But Mr. O'Brien found me a nuisance. Mr. O'Brien wasn't aggressive enough. We should have embarked on a policy of expansion. We have been slow in developing our rich land holdings in Culver City."

Levin's various charges were dismissed, and he was forced to back down. Most seriously, he was shown to have failed to include, in preparing his report, the returns on *Dr. Zhivago* and *How the West Was Won*. "My accountants overlooked it," he ruefully confessed. What they had overlooked was the fact that *Dr. Zhivago* was the fourth highest grossing picture in the industry's history.

By advertising Philip Levin's takeover bid, MGM avoided destruction: Levin wanted it pulled down and sold for real estate. But its future was, as late as 1971, still extremely shaky. Late in 1968 the company virtually fell apart, its only fiscal gain in a six-month period from film rentals and TV leasings. Even its recording division went $4 million into the red. Inevitably, Robert H. O'Brien was meted out the same punishment as Joseph R. Vogel before him: from being the golden boy of only a year earlier, he became chairman, that point of no return his predecessor had faced. In December, the important shareholder Edgar Bronfman assumed an advisory capacity, head of an executive board, and Louis F. (Bo) Polk became president. Under Polk, the company showed more than $35 million deficits in 1968, and the board demanded a new president. O'Brien, meanwhile, was forced out as chairman and retired to a life of fishing in the mountains.

Late in 1969, MGM passed into the hands of a new owner, a Las Vegas financier and hotel owner, Kirk Kerkorian. Polk, whose reign lasted only ten months, was ousted in November. In place of Polk, Kerkorian appointed James T. Aubrey, former president of CBS, who was still in charge by 1972 and was harassed by a number of lawsuits launched by directors who claimed interference with their films.

15

In the 1960s the urge to make pictures in Europe drastically increased. The much publicized need of studios to employ cheaper labor was only part of the cause; equally strong was the motivation of million-dollar players who needed the tax concessions that living away from home provided. In 1961 the alarm among labor unions became extremely widespread: John L. Dales, national executive secretary of the Screen Actors' Guild, was in continual conference with Eric Johnston of MPAA, and in mid-1961 the Hollywood AFL Film Council drafted and distributed to 1,200 unions a resolution condemning American stars and directors who chose to work abroad. All members were asked to boycott the films made by the traitors to America; few, as it turned out, actually heeded the call. Members of the Screen Cartoonists Guild experienced a 50 percent employment cut in 1962. The projectionists union was forced to agree to have only one man to each booth in theaters showing 35mm movies. It was not until 1964 that the runaway threat began to recede and—following a series of locally made box office hits, and the increase in the giant costs of foreign location production—something like the atmosphere of the old Hollywood temporarily re-emerged by 1965.

Walt Disney's *Mary Poppins* introduced Julie Andrews as the perfect embodiment of Pamela Travers' charming, flying nanny, in English settings cleverly realized under the supervision of a little-acknowledged English director, Robert Stevenson. George Cukor made *My Fair Lady,* a handsome, elegant, perhaps not sufficiently buoyant version of the enormously successful musical; Robert Wise's *Sound of Music* (seen by one woman sixty-seven times) was a glowing example of schmaltz, superbly tailored to the needs of a mass audience.

In 1964, Walter Mirisch announced that in future nearly all of his films would be made in Hollywood, and Al Zimbalist followed him. Martin Ransohoff's *The Sandpiper,* with the Burtons, was a depressing effort, but from labor's point of view it was very satisfactorily filmed on the California coast. By 1966 the industry was looking healthier than it had for a decade, with a 70 percent rise in Hollywood employment, and one success after another causing an authentic glow of excitement and confidence. The restaurants were again jammed at the lunch hour, the Sunset Strip area boomed (just before the age of the hippies), parties sparkled in Beverly Hills.

Formal craftsmanship had virtually disappeared in Hollywood by 1971. Laboratory standards fell as professional discipline collapsed. The majority of films—apart from the *drek* of sado-masochist and pornographic films with their thrashing bodies and lost, depressed, blotched faces—were predictably unpredictable, aggressively commercial, amateur works thrown together by the seemingly half-witted or near-psychotic. Films like *Little Murders* or *The Sporting Club* were as much symptoms of a chaotic and violent adolescent society as critiques of that society. Only very rare works—a *Patton*, politically ambiguous but recalling the 20th Century-Fox standards of craftsmanship of another era, or a *Five Easy Pieces*, pretentious but often vividly acted and written—served to remind one that Hollywood had at its worst maintained high technical standards, while new cinematographers like Laszlo Kovacs and William Fraker emerged to suggest that quality in camera work had not entirely vanished.

New directors of the sixties had somewhat shaky careers. A John Frankenheimer could emerge as a gifted social commentator, achieving in 1962 (his *annus mirabilis*) no less than three extraordinary works, *The Manchurian Candidate, Birdman of Alcatraz,* and his neglected, bitterly sad portrait of small-town American life *All Fall Down*. *Seven Days in May* and *Seconds,* made in 1963 and 1964, were powerful, dealing with the subjects of American political corruption and the national terror of age. Frankenheimer was a genuine American commentator. But as his personal wealth and importance increased, he acquired a fateful interest in Europe, carried away by the need to emulate Godard or Truffaut, and his talent disintegrated. The subject matter of *The Fixer,* Bernard Malamud's story of a political prisoner, was not unimportant, but Frankenheimer's treatment was disappointingly conventional; his *The Gypsy Moths,* about skydivers, with a middle-aged Burt Lancaster and Deborah Kerr embarrassingly repeating their *From Here to Eternity* oceanside nuzzle on a living-room couch, was nothing short of a disaster. So, too, were his quietly decent but ineffectual *I Walk the Line* and his *Extraordinary Seaman*.

Stanley Kramer, Theodore Flicker, and Sidney Lumet, all white hopes of the first half of the decade, tended to be regarded as the white elephants of the second. In their places, new directors like Robert Altman, Bob Rafelson, Monte Hellman, and Jim McBride stepped in. In 1971 it was too early to see whether these gifted men would, like their predecessors, merely take a comet's course and rapidly disappear.

One satisfactory feature of the new decade was the emergence of young executives, confirming the impression, growing steadily since 1968, that Hollywood could no longer be regarded as an old man's town. At Warners, Kenneth Hyman (until his resignation and departure for England) and Ted Ashley, at Paramount Bob Evans, at Universal Ned Tannen and Daniel Selznick—these vigorous men provided a new image to replace the familiar Hollywood look of a sunlit old folks' home. True, many veterans suffered, and employment problems became more acute. Arthur Miller, superb cinematographer of *How Green Was My Valley,* committed suicide because of acute distress at the sufferings of older members of his American Society of Cinematographers. While film history became a selling commodity and tape recorders whirred, taking down the words of the veterans, a whole new generation emerged that had barely heard of a Karl Struss or a Charles Rosher, still-living cameramen from Hollywood's past. Yet the change, tragic for some though it may have been, was healthy and inevitable.

Desperate efforts were made to unload studios. By 1970 Paramount was on the verge of being sold to the adjoining cemetery, where many of its famous lay buried (including Cecil B. De Mille), and moving what was left of its staff into a small office building in Beverly Hills. Personnel were fired, overseas offices closed or merged with other studios. After three years and $3 million James Aubrey canceled *Man's Fate,* MGM's giant production to have been made by Fred Zinnemann, and also shelved plans to make John Boorman's *Rosencrantz and Guildenstern Are Dead.* In the spring of 1970 MGM staged a massive auction of its past possessions: it looked to many visitors as though it were the last scene of *Citizen Kane,* with the spirits of Louis B. Mayer, Irving Thalberg, and Cedric Gibbons hovering over the treasures and detritus of a lost world. A distracted Adolph Green was heard to say, "I've just been ordered off sound stage twenty-seven because I don't have an identification tag." It seemed only appropriate that sound stage twenty-seven—scene of the auction itself—was where his and Betty Comden's captivating musical *Bandwagon* (and other Minnelli musicals, including *An American in Paris*) had been made. The auction ranged from the stupefying to the pathetic: endless anchors and ropes and chains, Clark Gable's trenchcoat and Judy Garland's *Wizard of Oz* shoes (which fetched $15,000), and, if you were really a glutton for punishment, a bed of nails (from *Kim*). It was, like the 20th Century-Fox auction which followed it in 1971, almost too perfectly symbolic of the end of an era.

The 1960s saw the merging of Joseph E. Levine's Embassy Pictures with Avco, a firm specializing in military and space travel equipment, as Avco–Embassy. Apart from ABC pictures, the new companies of Cinema Centre Films and Commonwealth United became prominent, the latter plagued by financial problems.

Transamerica—a diversified insurance and financing company—was a mammoth which had no difficulty in coolly acquiring 87 percent of United Artists stock in April, 1967. On April 20 the two companies held a joint luncheon at New York's Yale Club, presided over by John R. Beckett, president, Edward L. Scarff, vice-president of Transamerica, Robert S. Benjamin, chairman, Arthur B. Krim, president, Arnold Ricker, executive vice-president, and David V. Picker of United Artists. The atmosphere was enthusiastic, unmarked by the tension of the Gulf and Western–Paramount takeover; yet it was to be only four years before United Artists announced a net loss after taxes of $52 million for the year 1970, the largest single year loss in the history of the industry, exceeding even the $36 million loss of 20th Century-Fox.

While the studios were taken over one by one—leaving only Disney, Columbia, and 20th Century-Fox autonomous—it emerged more and more clearly that they were being kept alive by television production and successive sales of real estate, beginning with 20th Century-Fox's outright disposal of its backlot to the Century City project in the early 1960s. Their only major asset was their actual land, obtained many decades before.

Independent film-making did not quite mean what it suggested. True, a movie-maker could put long miles between himself and studio executives, shooting pictures on location as much for self-protection as for a need to show the life of the "real" America. But once back at the studio he was liable to run into major problems: studios that cut, tampered with, or otherwise emasculated projects they had financed and would sell to the theater chains, that added scenes sometimes handled by other directors. Often a studio would fail to sell a picture properly or release it at all. It might be less restricting for directors to operate under the new system than as a long-term studio employee, but often they were denied the right of final cut, or the right to supervise the processing or choose the laboratories, forced to see critics blaming them for a picture's inadequacies where once they would more confidently have blamed the studios.

Despite the fact though, life for a creative artist in Hollywood in the 1970s was a better one than it had been—provided, of course, that he could prove himself capable of making a studio large sums of money. The ability to make money remained the one and only yardstick of quality, and directors and actors, high on a project at its completion, would dismiss it six months later if the box office results were bad. The environment remained as pitiless as ever, allowing for no weakness, judging everyone in terms of his commerical value, measuring people's usefulness by the gold ounce. The squabbles, the tensions of studio executives hanging onto highly priced jobs by trembling fingertips, were still there. Hollywood hadn't really changed with the rise of the free-wheeling independent film, it had only become rejuvenated, grown its hair long, assumed love beads and learned to puff grass. The love religion in a 1970s Hollywood was a bitter joke, demanding a Nathanael West to do it justice. The sunshine still streamed down on Hollywood Boulevard, but the pullulating crowds seemed ever more desperate and ravaged, selling anything, including themselves, to make a buck. For all the speckless streets and gleaming white buildings, the suave attractions of Bel Air and Beverly Hills, the smart crowds in the Beverly Hills Polo Lounge, the martinis for breakfast and the muffins piled high with strawberry jam, Hollywood, like Los Angeles as a whole, was a desperate place. Directors like Robert Altman (*McCabe and Mrs. Miller*) and Dennis Hopper (*The Last Movie*) opted out altogether, fleeing to Vancouver and Taos respectively. Proof that it was now as cheap to make films on American home territory as it was in Europe seemed firmly established by 1971, but nobody could call the atmosphere relaxing. Against a single freak success like *Love Story*—which caused a crying mania equivalent to the dancing mania of the Middle Ages—could be set the monumental flops of almost all the college films of the 1969–70 period: the *Strawberry Statements* and the *Stanley Sweethearts*. Pay-TV—by which a picture could recoup its costs in a single night—seemed as remote as ever, opposed by powerful pressure groups that were stimulated by the exhibitors. The successes of *Airport* and the Disney films seemed to suggest that children and the Silent Majority were still the best audiences to aim for, but nobody really knew. By 1971 the stakes in the new Hollywood were as high as they had ever been, a studio executive could be made or broken by the public's unpredictable reactions. Only a fool would envy the Young Turks their kidney-shaped swimming pools in the years to come.